FORD CORSAIR

Illustrated Car Servicing Series for Owner Drivers

FORD CORSAIR 1500

(ALL MODELS FROM 1963–1965)

With 82 Illustrations

By

D. KABERRY

HAMLYN
LONDON · NEW YORK · SYDNEY · TORONTO

© The Hamlyn Publishing Group Ltd 1965

ISBN 0 600 42084 1

First Published 1965
Second impression 1965
Third impression 1968
Fourth impression 1969
Fifth impression 1972

THE HAMLYN PUBLISHING GROUP LIMITED
LONDON · NEW YORK · SYDNEY · TORONTO
Hamlyn House, Feltham, Middlesex, England

Printed and Bound in Great Britain by Cox & Wyman Ltd
London, Fakenham and Reading

PREFACE

MOTOR manufacturers all agree that for a car to give its ultimate in performance and reliability it must be regularly and correctly serviced. Almost half the work booked in by the majority of garages takes the form of manufacturer's schedule services and with high labour costs it is little wonder that many owners are carrying out their own servicing.

Whilst this is all very well when the work is carried out properly, some owners with no practical background whatsoever only serve to make their cars less reliable by doing jobs incorrectly. This is no fault of their own; it is due simply to the fact that they have no detailed instructions to follow – and this is where the present maintenance book comes to their assistance.

This book covers the Ford Corsair range – standard, de luxe and G.T. models produced up to September 1965 with the 1,500-c.c. in-line engine. The Corsair V4 models introduced at the 1965 Motor Show will be the subject of a separate book. It is based on the manufacturer's servicing schedules. The first few chapters tell the owner what tools and materials he needs, how to road test the vehicle, and sets out in full each service under its appropriate mileage. The subsequent chapters describe in full how each job contained in the servicing lists is carried out.

Illustrations are clear and precise, the text is easy to understand and contains the minimum of technical terms. It is a book for the untrained owner-driver which will enable him to tackle servicing procedure knowing that he is carrying it out in the correct, professional manner.

Grateful acknowledgment is made to the Ford Motor Company, Limited, for their assistance in providing illustrations and information.

CONTENTS

Chapter 1

INTRODUCTION

THIS book covers the Ford Consul Corsair models produced from October 1963 to September 1965. (The Corsair V4 models, in production from October 1965 to autumn 1970, will be the subject of a separate book).

The model range comprised the Standard, De Luxe and G.T. cars, all of which utilized a 1,500-c.c. engine, four-speed fully synchromesh gearbox and a hypoid rear axle, with disc brakes fitted to the front wheels. The G.T. car had a higher-powered engine, remote-control gearshift mounted in the centre console, extra instrumentation and full de-luxe specification including even coat hooks and assist straps. To cater for the improved performance, power-assisted brakes were fitted.

1. (*left*) CONSUL CORSAIR TWO-DOOR SALOON

2. (*right*) CONSUL CORSAIR G.T. FOUR-DOOR SALOON

3. INSTRUMENT PANEL AND CONTROLS ON G.T. MODEL
UP TO OCTOBER 1964

All models were available as two- or four-door versions and, in the body construction, use was made of double-skinned panels and glass-fibre insulation to provide sound deadening. Zero-torque locks were fitted to all doors to give easy, quiet closing; the rear-door locks on four-door cars also incorporate an overriding childproof device.

To complete the effortless motoring offered by these cars, the Standard and De Luxe versions were available with Borg-Warner automatic transmission.

INSTRUMENTS AND CONTROLS

The instruments and controls on all models of the Consul Corsair are basically the same, although on G.T. models a tachometer, ammeter and oil-pressure gauge are fitted as extra instrumentation.

The main instruments are incorporated in the speedometer cluster and these reading from left to right are fuel gauge, speedometer and water-temperature gauge. The fuel and temperature gauges are designed to eliminate oscillation when travelling. With these instruments, it takes approximately thirty seconds after switching on the ignition for the needles to establish their correct reading.

In addition to the main instruments, warning lights are also incorporated in the speedometer cluster, these again reading from left to right are as follows:

Left-hand direction-indicator arrow in the lower edge of the fuel gauge.

Generator or ignition-warning light – this is the red sector to the left of the odometer and is illuminated when the ignition is switched on and the generator is not charging the battery. This will be 'on' when ignition is switched on

4. INSTRUMENT PANEL AND CONTROLS ON G.T. MODEL FROM OCTOBER 1964

5. INSTRUMENT PANEL AND CONTROLS ON STANDARD AND DE LUXE MODELS
FROM OCTOBER 1964

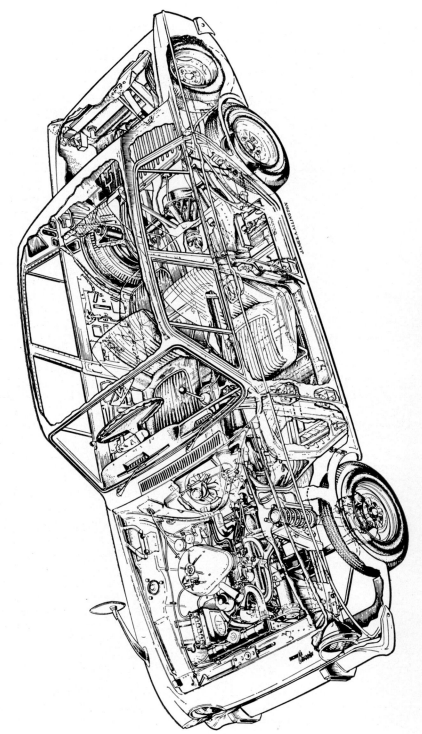

6. CUT-AWAY VIEW OF CONSUL CORSAIR

with the engine stationary, or running at idling speed, and should go out as the engine speed increases. Any time this light remains on regardless of engine speed, the charging circuit should be checked as this indicates that the generator is not charging the battery. If the light does not come on when the ignition is switched on, it may be due to a defective bulb, this should be checked otherwise (except on G.T.) there is no indication of any defect which may develop in the charging circuit.

Oil-pressure warning light (except G.T.) – this is coloured green and is located to the right of the odometer. This should be on when the ignition is switched on and the engine stationary; it may flicker when idling but should be out at speeds above idling. If the light remains or comes on with the engine running above idling speed, the engine should be switched off immediately to determine the reason for the low oil pressure.

Headlamp main-beam warning light – this is blue and is on when the headlamp main beams are switched on, and off when the headlamps are dipped.

Right-hand direction-indicator arrow in the lower edge of the temperature gauge.

The appropriate indicator-warning lights should flash when the direction indicators are switched on. If these flash above their normal rate, or both are illuminated together, it shows a fault in the direction-indicator circuit and the bulbs should be checked for damaged filaments or poor contacts; where the bulbs are all right, the flasher unit should be replaced.

On G.T. models, the main instrument panel is identical to the Standard and De Luxe but, in addition, an electrically driven tachometer is mounted on the steering column and an ammeter and oil-pressure gauge are fitted in the console over the remote gear-change linkage up to October 1964. From this date, the tachometer is fitted in the console and the ammeter and oil-pressure gauge are mounted in place of the ashtray (to the left of the instrument panel). The ashtray is now fitted in the centre console.

Illumination bulbs are fitted in the main instrument panel and also in each of the auxiliary instruments on G.T. models; up to October 1964, no separate panel-lamp switch is

fitted, these being switched on whenever the side-lights are on. From this date, a separate panel-lamp switch is fitted on the lower edge of the fascia, which operates in conjunction with the side-lamp switch.

The following controls are fitted on the lower fascia panel.

Choke Control

The choke control is fitted on the left of the panel and is marked with a vane diagram on the face of the knob, and gives a progressively richer mixture as the control is pulled outwards. The control can be locked in any position by turning the knob to the right, although it should be released and pushed in as soon as possible after starting the engine.

Windscreen-wiper Control

The windscreen-wiper control is fitted on the right of the lower panel, with a diagram of the wiper arc on the knob face. A variable-speed wiper motor is fitted. This is switched on by turning the knob clockwise, further movement of the knob in this direction will increase the wiper motor speed. On De Luxe and G.T. models which are fitted with a windscreen washer, the pump is incorporated in the wiper-motor switch and is operated by pushing the control knob inwards. The knob is returned to the normal position automatically, at the same time recharging the pump.

Ignition and Starter Switch

This is located on the extreme right of the lower fascia panel. Turning the switch key clockwise will switch on the ignition and any auxiliary circuits which may be wired through this switch. Turning the key further clockwise against spring pressure will switch on the starter motor. If the key is turned anti-clockwise, the auxiliary circuits will be switched on, but not the ignition circuit. This prevents overloading the battery and over-heating the ignition circuit when the car is stationary. A radio should be wired through this position.

Lighting Switch

On models up to October 1964, the lighting switch is the outer switch of the two mounted on

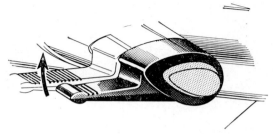

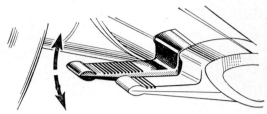

7. LIGHTING SWITCH AND HORN BUTTON – UP TO OCTOBER 1964

The shorter, outer lever on steering column is the lighting switch and is off when horizontal. Moving switch in direction of arrow first turns on side and tail lights. In next position of switch, all lights are on with headlamps dipped. In final forward position, all lights are on with headlamps on main beams.

The horn button is located in the end of the lighting switch.

8. DIRECTION-INDICATOR SWITCH – UP TO OCTOBER 1964

The longer, inner lever on the steering column is the direction-indicator switch. Move the switch lever upwards to operate the left-hand flashing indicators and downwards for operation of the right-hand flashing indicators.

The direction indicators are self-cancelling and only operate when the ignition is switched on.

the right-hand side of the steering column. When the lever is horizontal all lights are off. When the lever is moved forward into the first position the side, rear and instrument-panel lights are on; in the next forward position dipped headlamps are switched on, and when fully forward, the headlamp main beams are on. The instrument-panel lights are on at all times the side-lights are on, no separate switch is fitted for these.

From October 1964, the lighting switch is fitted to the right of the upper instrument panel; headlamp dip, direction indicators and flasher are controlled by a single lever mounted on the right of the steering column. A panel-lamp

switch is also fitted on the lower edge of the fascia.

Direction-indicator Switch

On models up to October 1964, the direction-indicator switch is the inner, longer lever on the steering column: when moved forward it operates the left-hand direction-indicator lights and the right-hand ones when moved backwards. On Standard models, the horn button is fitted in the centre of the headlamp switch at the outer end of the bracket. On De Luxe and G.T. models, a horn ring is fitted and this button is used to operate the headlamp flasher. When the ignition is switched on and the button depressed, the headlamp main-beam filaments will be switched on. This of course is ineffective if the main beams are already switched on by the lighting switch.

From October 1964, a single lever on the steering column controls the direction indicators, headlamp, dip and flasher. The lever operates the direction indicators when moved in the normal plane of the steering wheel and switches the headlights to main beam when depressed away from the wheel. To dip the lights, the lever must be pulled towards the wheel. On Standard models, the horn button is mounted in the end. A headlamp flasher is fitted so that the headlamp main beam can be switched on any time the ignition is on; this is operated

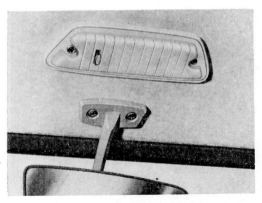

9. INTERIOR LIGHT MOUNTED ON WINDSCREEN HEADER PANEL

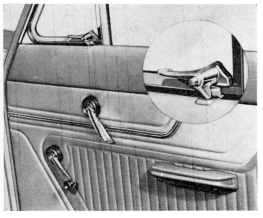

10. REAR-DOOR LOCK WITH CHILD-PROOF SAFETY CATCH

Moving the safety catch downwards (shown at bottom of illustration) before closing the door, will prevent the door being opened by the inside handle.

11. FRONT-DOOR CONTROLS

The lower handle regulates window opening. Move upper handle forwards to lock door and upwards to open door. Inset shows enlarged view of vent window control.

by lifting the lever towards the steering wheel against spring tension. The lever returns to its normal position when released.

This lever can be depressed or raised when it has already been moved to operate the indicators, and, conversely, can be moved to operate the indicators when depressed or raised.

Interior Light

The interior light is mounted on the windscreen header panel and operates in conjunction with the courtesy switches in the front-door

pillars. The switch lever protrudes through the front of the lamp lens and has three positions. In the up position, the lamp is controlled by the courtesy switches being switched on when either front door is opened and off when the door is closed. In the centre position the lamp is permanently off, whilst in the down position the lamp is permanently on.

Locks

The doors are fitted with zero-torque locks to give easy closing, which are operated externally by push buttons incorporated in the door handles. A locking cylinder operated by the ignition key is fitted to the driver's door only.

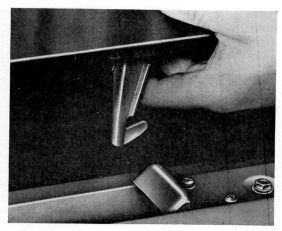

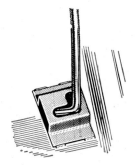

13. BONNET-SUPPORT STAY

The bonnet is supported in the open position by locating the stay in the bracket on the engine side of the wing.

12. BONNET-LOCK SAFETY CATCH

14. COMBINED VENTILATOR AND HEATER
CONTROLS

To lock this door, insert the key and turn it clockwise approximately a quarter turn. After locking the door return the key to the vertical position to withdraw it. The door is unlocked by turning the key the same amount anti-clockwise. The other doors must be locked by moving the internal handle fully forwards, although the handle will then return to its normal position.

Child-proof locks are fitted on the rear doors of four-door cars. On these cars a small lever can be seen protruding through the rear edge of the door when it is open – moving the lever downwards before closing the door will prevent it being opened by operating the inside handle. If the lever is moved upwards, the doors can be opened from the inside in the normal manner.

Vent windows are fitted in the front doors, the handles of these are self-locking when pushed fully downwards. To release them, depress the plunger in the centre of the handle at the same time turning the handle upwards.

On two-door cars, the rear side windows hinge outwards, being operated by an over-centre catch. When closing these, always ensure that the handle is pressed hard down to lock the windows.

The luggage-boot lid is self-locking and is counter-balanced by two torsion bars. The lock is operated by the ignition key and is released by turning the key clockwise.

The bonnet is unlocked internally by pulling the control marked 'HOOD' on the extreme right below the instrument panel. The bonnet will then be lifted sufficiently to allow the safety-catch to be pushed sideways to fully release the bonnet. The bonnet must be supported in the open position by the stay clipped inside it. Release the stay from its clips and locate the free end in the bracket on side of the engine compartment.

Heater or Ventilator Controls

Either a fresh-air heater or a ventilator is fitted to the Consul Corsair, the controls being located in the centre of the upper fascia panel. In the case of the fresh-air heater, two controls are fitted, the upper lever controls the temperature of the incoming air and the lower one the distribution of the air to the car interior, or to the windscreen. The lower lever also controls a two-speed fan – pulling the lever out to the first notch switches on the fan, the speed being increased by pulling the lever to the second notch.

No water valve is fitted to the heater so that even when the upper lever is on the cold position, the temperature of the air entering the car will be above the atmospheric temperature due to the cooling water circulation through the unit.

If required, the heater water supply can be turned off by a tap in the cylinder head. To turn off the water, turn the tap so that the line on the square shank is at right angles to the body of the tap.

The ventilator lever, where fitted, controls the distribution of fresh air. With the lever in the central position air is directed to the windscreen and with the lever on the extreme right, air is directed into the car interior.

Cigarette Lighter

Where a cigarette lighter is fitted, this is to the left of the heater or ventilator controls. The lighter is automatic – after pushing the element in to make contact, it automatically 'pops out' of the socket when it is hot. The socket is illuminated whenever the side-lights are on.

Seat Adjustment

The bench or individual type front seats are adjustable fore and aft. The control on the bench seat must be moved towards the outside of the car to unlock the seat. The individual seats are released by pressing the control down.

GENERAL DATA TABLE

Engine

Bore	80·96 mm.
Stroke	72·75 mm.
Capacity	1,498 c.c.
Compression ratio:	
H.C. standard engine	8·3:1
L.C. standard engine	7·0:1
H.C. G.T. engine..	9·0:1
Brake horse power:	
H.C. standard engine	59½ at 4,600 r.p.m.
L.C. standard engine	56 at 4,700 r.p.m.
H.C. G.T. engine..	78 at 5,200 r.p.m.
Firing order	1, 2, 4, 3

Valve clearance (hot):

Standard Engine

Inlet valve ..	0·010 in.
Exhaust valve ..	0·017 in.

G.T. Engine

Inlet valve ..	0·014 in.
Exhaust valve ..	0·021 in.

Engine Lubrication

Sump capacity ..	6¾ pt., 7½ pts. after Dec. 1964 (includes approx. ½ pt. for filter)
Lubricant	SAE.20W (summer and winter)

Cooling System

Capacity	11 pt. + 2 pt. if heater is fitted.
Radiator-cap pressure	10 lb./sq. in.
Fan	11-in. dia. – two blade

Fuel System

Tank capacity ..	8 gallons
Fuel grade:	
H.C. engine ..	Premium grade
L.C. engine ..	Regular grade

Standard Engine

Carburetter type ..	Zenith 33VN2
Main jet	92
Main air-correction jet	112
Idling jet	55
Accelerator pump jet	50
Choke-tube diameter	29 mm.

G.T. Engine

Carburetter type ..	Weber 28/36 DCD dual-barrel, two choke tubes per barrel

	Primary	Secondary
Choke-tube diameter	26 mm.	27 mm.
Auxiliary choke-tube diameter	4·5	4·5
Main jet	140	155
Air-correction jet ..	230	180
Slow-running jet ..	50	70
Starter petrol jet ..	190	
Starter air-correction jet	100	
Accelerator pump jet	60	

Ignition System

Ignition timing:	
Standard engine ..	8° b.t.d.c.
G.T. engine ..	10° b.t.d.c.
Contact-breaker gap..	0·014 to 0·016 in.
Spark plugs:	
Standard engine ..	Motorcraft AG3
G.T. engine ..	Motorcraft AG2
Plug gaps	0·023 to 0·028 in.

Clutch

Release-arm free movement	0·1 in.
Disc diameter ..	7·25 in.

Gearbox

Oil capacity	1¾ pt.
Grade of lubricant ..	SAE.80 E.P. gear oil

Gear Ratios

First	3·543 to 1
Second	2·396 to 1
Third	1·412 to 1
Top	1·000 to 1
Reverse	3·963 to 1

Rear Axle

Ratio	3·9:1 (4·125:1 optional, except G.T.)
Lubricant	SAE.90 Hypoid oil

Steering Gear

Ratio	15 to 1
Lubricant	SAE.90 E.P. gear oil

Brakes

Front disc dia. ..	9½ in.
Rear drum size ..	9 × 1¾ in.

Tyres

Tyre size	5·60–13
Pressure, lb./sq. in.:	
Standard and De Luxe	22
G.T., front/rear ..	24/26
G.T. with sustained high speeds, front/ rear	28/30

Dimensions

Wheelbase	8 ft. 5 in.
Length	14 ft. 8½ in.
Width..	5 ft. 3½ in.
Height (unladen) ..	4 ft. 9½ in.
Turning circle (swept)	36 ft. 6 in.

Chapter 2

ROAD TESTING FOR PERFORMANCE

IN time, as slight wear takes place, the settings and adjustments made to the engine and other components will change. This variation in setting will affect the performance of the car slightly at first, but if not corrected the deterioration in performance will increase. This gradual falling off in performance may not be apparent, particularly if the driver is operating the car every day and very often not until a similar car is driven, or some event on the road brings his attention to it, is this noticed.

To ensure that the car is operating at peak form, it will be found helpful to carry out a test run occasionally; the ideal time being after the 5,000-mile service has been carried out. This will serve two purposes; firstly, to check the vehicle and secondly, to check the standard of work which has been carried out.

Choice of Test Route

To establish the performance standard, choose a suitable route with a good stretch of level road, if possible, so that both acceleration and maximum speeds can be checked. These should be checked travelling in both directions to establish a mean figure, so that variations in road conditions and wind can be taken into account. If local conditions do not permit the car to be driven at maximum speed, this is not particularly important as the acceleration tests will show whether the engine is developing maximum power or not.

Road test figures published in motoring journals can be used as a guide to the performance to expect, but it should be borne in mind that these have been established by professionals and different driving techniques can materially affect the results. Acceleration figures from rest quoted in these tests are the best times that can be established making the fastest possible start from rest and, wherever possible, changing up on a full throttle. Many owners may not feel inclined to treat their car in this manner and naturally will not obtain these performance figures. Once the owner has established his own figures, using his own driving method, these can be used as a yardstick for all future tests.

It may be that the car is operated in a hilly district, where level stretches of road are not available to make these tests. If this is so, the performances can be established on a known hill and this used as a measure. Notice at what point it is necessary to change down, the maximum speed and in which gear the climb is completed; any falling off in performance will have a marked effect on these and will be easily noticeable.

Never try to establish performance figures on a new car, as it is not until a few thousand miles have been covered that all moving parts are fully run in and the maximum performance can be obtained. Similarly, changes in weather conditions will produce changes in performance; on a cool, damp day, the performance will be better than on a hot, dry one, due to the heavier fuel and air change drawn into the cylinders under these conditions.

Before making any tests, first check that the tyres are inflated to the correct pressure, then drive the car for a few miles to enable the engine to reach its normal working temperature. If acceleration times are to be made, an observer equipped with a stop-watch must be carried.

ACCELERATION TESTS

To check acceleration times from a standing start, say for the range 0–40 m.p.h., start the watch immediately the clutch is engaged and with the car accelerating hard all the time, stop the watch when 40 m.p.h. is reached. Do not ease the throttle pedal as 40 is approached, but accelerate past this, releasing the throttle only after the watch is stopped. As stated previously, published figures for standing-start acceleration are the best that can be obtained regardless of the smoothness of take-off and gear changing and figures obtained by the average driver may vary considerably from these.

Acceleration Times

The following are average acceleration times for the De Luxe saloon; these of course will be improved on by the G.T. model:

M.P.H.	Top Gear (sec.)	Third Gear (sec.)
20–40	11·2	7·3
30–50	10·5	8·2
40–60	12·0	9·3

The most satisfactory check for the owner-driver is a timed check over any speed range, say 30–60 m.p.h. in third or top gear. To make the test, engage the appropriate gear well below the lowest speed and then with full throttle held throughout the test, check the time taken over the selected speed range. This eliminates any variation due to gear change or starting technique. The test can be made several times, travelling in opposite directions, so that a mean figure can be established.

FUEL-CONSUMPTION TESTS

Fuel-consumption tests are made using an accurately measured quantity of fuel and carefully checking the distance over which this is consumed. The most satisfactory way for the owner-driver is to check the amount of fuel used and the mileage covered over any desired period; naturally, the longer the period the more accurate the check will be. If a check is made over each consecutive month a reliable average can be established and any wide variations from this may be taken as an indication of some minor adjustment, provided of course that operating conditions are the same throughout.

When making a fuel-consumption check in this manner, completely fill the tank at the beginning and end of the test to enable the fuel to be accurately measured.

Fuel consumption is one of the most contentious topics amongst motorists and many factors should be taken into account before any action is taken. A car which is driven from home two or three miles to the station, left all day and driven back at night will have a heavy fuel consumption, as under this treatment the engine never reaches normal working temperature, and its maximum efficiency. On the other hand, the same car on a long run may give a return approaching forty miles per gallon. Similarly, stop/start work or operating in heavy traffic will increase the fuel consumption and bring about wide variations on identical vehicles operating under different conditions.

The onus of obtaining the best fuel consumption is on the driver. Violent acceleration or high speeds in the intermediate gears or last-minute braking rather than rolling up to an obstruction, all increase fuel consumption. To get the best figures, accelerate from rest smoothly, change into a higher gear at a reasonable road speed and allow the car to build up gradually to the desired cruising speed. Once this has been reached it will be found that the throttle pedal can be eased back considerably whilst still maintaining the same road speed. Always keep the tyres inflated to the correct pressure as under-inflation will increase rolling resistance which will only be paid for by increased fuel consumption.

B

Chapter 3

ROUTINE MAINTENANCE

TO obtain maximum efficiency from the car, it must be serviced regularly. This servicing has a two-fold function: (*a*) lubrication to minimize wear on all working parts and (*b*) preventive maintenance to keep components operating efficiently and so eliminate unnecessary breakdowns.

The steering joints are pre-packed and operate in plastic seats, the drive-shaft (propeller shaft) universal joints are also pre-packed and sealed so there are no grease-gun points to be serviced.

MAINTENANCE SCHEDULE

In addition to daily and weekly checks, servicing should be carried out at the first 500 miles, every 5,000 miles and every 15,000 miles. The servicing schedule is listed below and full details of carrying out all these operations are given in the appropriate chapters. The first 500-mile service is normally a free service by the supplying Dealer, but details are given below if for any reason this cannot be done.

Daily

Check oil and water levels.

Weekly

Check battery electrolyte level.
Check tyre pressures.
Check brake- and clutch-fluid reservoir levels.

At First 500 Miles

Engine
Tighten cylinder-head bolts.
Check valve clearances.
Check fan-belt tension.
Check for oil and water leaks.

Fuel System
Clean fuel-pump sediment bowl and filter.
Adjust carburetter slow running.

Electrical System
Check battery electrolyte level.
Adjust distributor contact-breaker points.

Gearbox and Clutch
Check gearbox oil level.
Check clutch-fluid reservoir level.
Check clutch adjustment at release arm.

Steering
Check steering-box oil level.
Check front-wheel bearing adjustment.
Check front-wheel toe-in.

Brakes
Check brake-fluid reservoir level.
Adjust brakes if necessary.

Rear Axle
Check rear-axle oil level.
Check rear-spring U-bolts.

General
Check tightness of all wheel nuts.
Lubricate locks, hinges, throttle linkage, etc.

Every 5,000 Miles

All the points checked at the first 500-mile service should be repeated every 5,000 miles except it is not necessary to tighten the cylinder-head bolts after the 500-mile check. The gearbox oil should be changed at the first 5,000-mile service only; at subsequent services it is only necessary to check the oil level.

The following additional work should be carried out.

Engine
Change engine oil.
Change oil filter.
Clean gauze in oil filler cap.

Fuel System
Clean air cleaner.

Electrical System
Clean spark plugs.

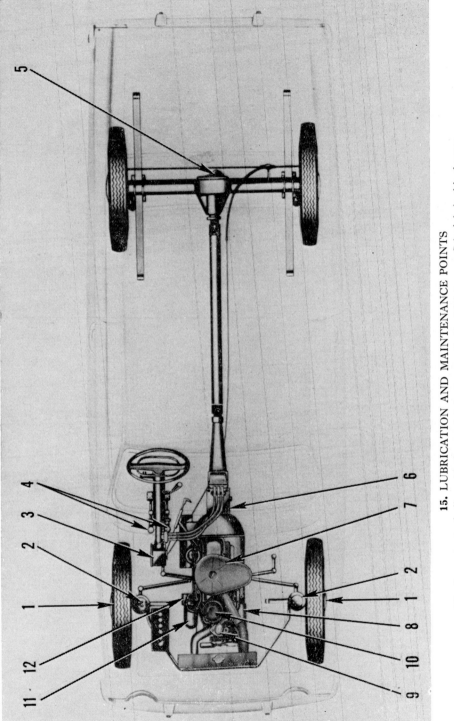

15. LUBRICATION AND MAINTENANCE POINTS

The frequency in dealing with these points is given under the Maintenance Schedule in this chapter.

1. Front-wheel bearings
2. Front suspension unit (shock absorbers)
3. Steering box
4. Brake and clutch master cylinders
5. Rear axle
6. Gearbox
7. Air cleaner
8. Generator
9. Oil-level dipstick
10. Oil-filler cap
11. Oil filter
12. Distributor

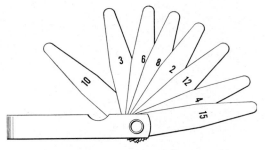

Set of feeler gauges.

Spark-plug spanner and tommy bar.

Set of open-ended spanners (A.F.)

Pair of pliers

Polythene battery filler for topping-up the battery with distilled water.

Small screwdriver.

Large screwdriver.

Medium-size Phillips-type screwdriver.

Handy pocket-size tyre-pressure gauge.

16. TOOLS FOR ROUTINE MAINTENANCE

Electrical System
   Lubricate distributor.
   Lubricate generator rear bearing.
Brakes
   Inspect front-brake pads and rear-brake shoes.
   Lubricate handbrake relay lever.
Steering
   Examine steering-joint plastic gaiters for damage.
   Check security of crossmember retaining bolts.

Every 15,000 Miles

In addition to the normal 5,000-mile service, top up front shock absorbers, also the front hub bearings should be cleaned and repacked with fresh grease.

TOOLS AND ACCESSORIES

If an owner proposes to carry out his own maintenance it is essential that he be equipped with the correct tools to carry out the work correctly and efficiently. The first essential is a good set of spanners; all nuts and bolts on these cars are of the A.F. size and the spanners should cover a range from $\frac{7}{16}$ in. A.F. to $\frac{3}{4}$ in. A.F. Open-ended spanners are quite satisfactory, although it will be found for some operations, such as cylinder-head bolt tightening, a ring spanner or socket may be better. Never make do with spanners of the incorrect size or shifting spanners as these may slip causing damage to the nut or bolt-head and the operator's knuckles.

A small squirt oil-can can be used for topping up front shock absorbers, and this should be filled with the correct shock absorber fluid and kept exclusively for this operation. Another oil-can will be necessary for lubrication of the generator rear bearing and other normal oil-can points.

The rear springs should be sprayed with penetrating oil and this is now obtainable as an aerosol pack which greatly simplifies this job. At the same time, the aerosol pack enables awkward or inaccessible points to be lubricated easily.

The owner should also equip himself with two screwdrivers; one of these should have a cross-head end, a set of feeler blades and a good pair of pliers.

Have a container of at least one-gallon capacity to drain the oil into. Also one or two smaller containers will be found useful for washing various parts, as necessary.

A small syringe will be found useful for topping up the gearbox and rear-axle oil levels.

Much of the work has to be done under the car, so that a small trolley jack or a pair of portable ramps will be found useful so that the front or rear ends of the car can be lifted off the ground. If a jack is used, take care to put supports under the car before working under it in case of failure of the jack.

RECOMMENDED LUBRICANTS

The following list gives the lubricants for correct maintenance.

Engine	.. ..	SAE.20 (summer and winter).
Gearbox	.. ..	SAE.80 E.P. gear oil.
Rear axle	.. ..	SAE.90 hypoid oil.
Steering box	..	SAE.90 E.P. gear oil.
Front suspension	..	Shock-absorber fluid M100502-E.
Brake and clutch master cylinders		Fluid ME3833-E.

It is essential that the brake and clutch cylinder fluid is kept clean and is not contaminated with mineral oil. The precautions to be taken when topping up these units are covered in Chapters 8 and 12 and should be strictly observed. Similarly, distilled water should be kept only in an airtight glass container.

SPARES

Provided that the car is maintained correctly there will be little likelihood of roadside breakdowns occurring. The following spares may be carried with advantage, however, in the event of this happening:

A spare set of spark plugs, cleaned and correctly gapped. These should be kept in their own containers to prevent accidental damage in storage.

A set of contact-breaker points and condenser.

A spare fan belt.

Replacement side and rear lamp bulbs should always be carried in the car, so that these may be replaced immediately a failure occurs.

Chapter 4

ENGINE

THE engine used in the Consul Corsair Standard and De Luxe models is a four-cylinder overhead-valve unit of 1,498-c.c. capacity. The cylinder-bore diameter is 80·96 mm., the piston stroke being 72·75 mm. It is available with either low- or high-compression cylinder heads, the high-compression version being standard.

The G.T. car is fitted with a high-performance version of this engine. The principle changes are: modified camshaft; larger exhaust valves; reshaped combustion chambers in cylinder head; four-branch aluminium inlet manifold fitted with a twin-choke downdraught carburetter; and a four-branch exhaust manifold. The compression ratio has been raised and to cater for the increased power output, lead/bronze or copper/lead main-bearing liners are fitted.

Apart from these variations, the construction and servicing of the engine units is similar in all cases. Details of these and the variations on any particular engine are given in this chapter.

The valves are mounted vertically in the cylinder head, the valve guides being cast in the cylinder head. The inlet-valve heads are slightly larger in diameter than those of the exhaust valves to give better charging of the cylinders. The cast-steel crankshaft is supported in five main bearings and these and the connecting-rod big ends are fitted with replaceable steel-backed liners. A single-roller chain drives the camshaft from the crankshaft and a spring-loaded snail-cam chain tensioner is bolted to the sump flange. The camshaft is located on the right-hand side of the cylinder block and operates the valve rockers through tappets and push rods. A skew gear, cut on the forward end of the camshaft, drives both the distributor and oil pump; an eccentric at the rear end of the camshaft operates the mechanical fuel pump.

The pistons are of the autothermic type, fitted with two compression and one oil-control ring. The fully-floating piston pins (gudgeon pins) are retained by circlips fitted in the piston-pin bores. The oil pump is mounted externally and is incorporated in the head of the full-flow oil-filter unit.

A thermostat is located in the cylinder-head outlet. The water pump is bolted to the front face of the cylinder block and is driven in tandem with the generator (dynamo) by a V-belt from the crankshaft.

To ensure maximum engine life, maintenance should be carried out at the specified mileage periods. Full details of the necessary maintenance are given later in this section.

Oil-pressure Warning Light

An oil-pressure gauge is fitted to the G.T. model and an oil-pressure warning light is incorporated in the instrument panel on other models. This light is operated by a pressure switch located in the cylinder block and should be ON when the ignition is switched on with the engine stationary. The light may flicker momentarily when the engine is running at idling speed but should be OFF when the engine is running at normal speed. If the light remains ON permanently, the engine must not be operated. Should this light come on when the engine is running or remain on after the engine has started, switch off immediately and check the engine oil level. If the oil level is correct, further checks will have to be made to determine the loss of oil pressure. The causes of low oil pressure are given later in this chapter but it must be stressed that, to carry out the

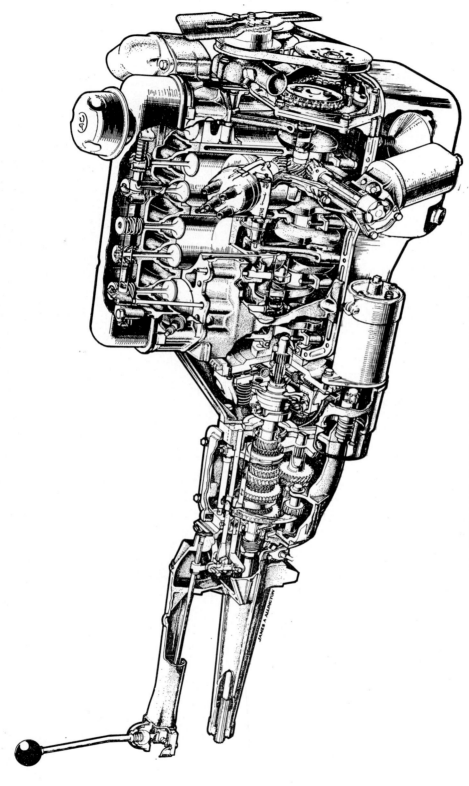

17. CUT-AWAY VIEW OF ENGINE, CLUTCH AND GEARBOX

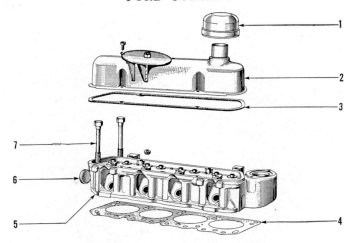

18. CYLINDER-HEAD ASSEMBLY

1. Oil-filler cap
2. Valve-rocker cover
3. Rocker-cover gasket
4. Cylinder-head gasket

5. Cylinder head
6. Core plug
7. Cylinder-head securing bolt (10 off)

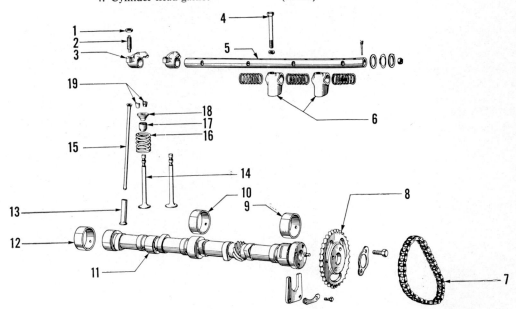

19. VALVE-OPERATING MECHANISM

1. Locknut
2. Valve-clearance adjusting screw.
3. Valve rocker
4. Bracket-securing bolt
5. Rocker shaft
6. Rocker brackets or pedestals

7. Timing chain
8. Camshaft sprocket
9. Front camshaft bearing
10. Centre camshaft bearing
11. Camshaft
12. Rear camshaft bearing
13. Tappet

14. Valve
15. Push rod
16. Valve spring
17. Valve oil-seal
18. Valve-spring retainer
19. Split collets

Note. – The umbrella-type valve oil-seal (17) must be fitted with the open end downwards.

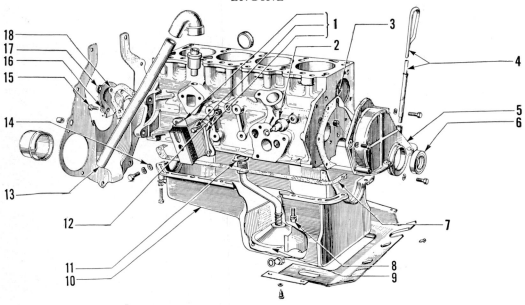

20. CYLINDER BLOCK AND SUMP COMPONENTS

1. Engine mounting
2. Oil-pressure switch
3. Timing cover gasket
4. Oil-level dipstick
5. Timing cover

6. Oil seal
7. Oil-sump gasket
8. Sump-securing bolt
9. Gauze strainer
10. Sump

11. Oil-suction pipe tab washer
12. Plug
13. Crankcase ventilation tube

14. Engine-mounting bolt washer
15. Securing bolt
16. Spring washer
17. Camshaft end plate
18. Gasket

21. CRANKSHAFT, FLYWHEEL AND PISTONS

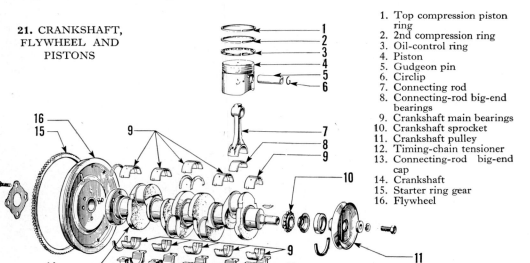

1. Top compression piston ring
2. 2nd compression ring
3. Oil-control ring
4. Piston
5. Gudgeon pin
6. Circlip
7. Connecting rod
8. Connecting-rod big-end bearings
9. Crankshaft main bearings
10. Crankshaft sprocket
11. Crankshaft pulley
12. Timing-chain tensioner
13. Connecting-rod big-end cap
14. Crankshaft
15. Starter ring gear
16. Flywheel

majority of these checks, the engine must be dismantled.

ENGINE LUBRICATION SYSTEM

The engine is lubricated by oil fed at a high pressure from the oil pump. Two types of pump may be fitted to these engines – either an eccentric bi-rotor or rotating vane-type pump.

An oil-pressure relief valve is incorporated in the oil pump, to prevent excessively high pressures being built up, particularly when starting the engine from cold.

Oil is drawn from the sump through a gauze strainer to the oil pump. From the oil pump, the oil is forced at high pressure through a full-flow oil filter before entering the main oil gallery. A relief valve is incorporated in the head of the filter, so that if the element becomes excessively blocked, oil can by-pass the filter to lubricate the engine.

Drillings from the main oil gallery supply oil to the main bearings and the camshaft bearings. Drillings in the crankshaft feed the big-end bearings from the main bearings; a small

drilling in each big-end bearing allows a jet of oil to lubricate the cylinder walls.

A flat machined on the front camshaft journal allows an intermittent feed of oil to pass through drillings in the cylinder block to the front rocker-shaft support thence via the hollow rocker shaft to the valve rockers. Drillings in each valve rocker feed oil to the valve and push-rod ends. The timing gears are lubricated by a constant bleed from a short oil gallery fed direct by the oil pump. The oil-pressure switch or gauge union is also located in this short gallery.

Normal oil pressure is 30–40 lb/sq. in. Where no pressure gauge is fitted and it is felt necessary to check the oil pressure, this can be done by unscrewing the pressure switch from the cylinder block and substituting an oil-pressure gauge in this position. The warning light located on the dashboard is extinguished when the oil pressure is above 7–9 lb/sq. in. The grade of engine oil to be used is SAE.20W for both summer and winter use, although a multigrade oil falling in this classification is also approved for use in these engines.

To ensure maximum engine life and minimum wear, only a good-quality engine oil should be used. Poor-quality oils may cause gumming of the piston rings with consequent loss of power, may be too thin when hot so causing poor lubrication, or may be excessively thick and gummy at low temperatures, which can give rise to difficult starting.

Many modern engine oils contain additives and have some detergent properties; these oils tend to be discoloured soon after being put into use. Because the oil has become discoloured, it should not be assumed that it is unfit for service. On the other hand, however, a careful check should be made of this condition and if it is found to be excessively contaminated through any reason, the engine oil should be drained and the oil filter changed regardless of engine mileage. If for any reason the oil has been contaminated by water leaking from the cooling system, it is advisable to flush out the engine before refilling the sump with fresh engine oil. This is particularly important if anti-freeze is in use as anti-freeze contamination will cause excessive sludging of the engine oil.

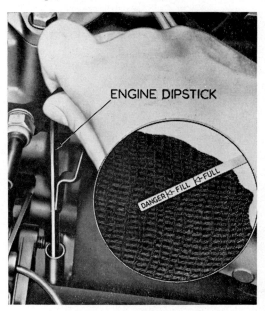

ENGINE DIPSTICK

DANGER FILL FULL

22. OIL-LEVEL DIPSTICK LOCATED AT LEFT-HAND SIDE OF ENGINE

Never allow the oil level to fall into the 'Danger' area marked on the dipstick.

ENGINE MAINTENANCE SCHEDULE

The engine maintenance should be carried out at the following periods:

Daily. Check engine oil level.

At First 500 Miles. Check cylinder-head bolt tightness and valve clearances.

Every 5,000 Miles. Drain and renew engine oil, change the oil-filter element and clean the breather incorporated in the oil-filler cap. Check valve clearances.

23. ENGINE OIL FILLER AND CAP MOUNTED ON VALVE-ROCKER COVER

It is only necessary to remove the filler cap in order to add oil to the engine.

The filler cap also incorporates a ventilator which allows fresh air to pass into the engine crankcase. The cap and gauze should be cleaned every 5,000 miles by first washing the cap in petrol, and then re-oiling the gauze; shake off any surplus oil before refitting the cap.

ENGINE LUBRICATION MAINTENANCE

The engine oil level should be checked daily with the car standing on level ground. To do this pull out the dipstick (see Fig. 22) and wipe off the oil. Replace the dipstick in its tube making sure that it is pushed right home and then withdraw it, the oil level should then be within the section marked 'FILL'. If necessary add oil of the correct grade to bring the oil level up to the 'FULL' mark. Do not overfill the engine as this oil will be lost. If the oil level falls within the area of the dipstick marked 'DANGER' the engine should not be run until the oil level has been brought up to the 'FULL' mark. When replacing the dipstick make sure that it is pushed right down into its tube.

Every 5,000 Miles

Every 5,000 miles, the engine oil should be changed and the oil-filter element renewed. It is advisable to carry out this operation when the engine is hot as the engine oil will flow more freely and drain off much easier. Place a container of at least 8 pints capacity under the engine sump and unscrew the drain plug. When all the oil has drained off wipe the surface of the sump, check that a copper washer is fitted to the sump plug and refit the plug, tightening it securely.

Place a container on the ground under the oil-filter body to catch any oil which may be lost from the filter when it is removed. Unscrew the centre bolt located in the head of the filter and detach the oil-filter body and the element. Remove the rubber sealing-ring located in the oil-filter head, remove and discard the old oil-filter element and thoroughly wash out the filter body. A new rubber sealing-ring is supplied with each replacement element and this should now be fitted in the groove in the head of the oil-filter body.

When refitting this ring, locate it in the groove at four points and gradually push it home. Do not start at one point and work round the groove or the ring may be stretched and you may have difficulty in fitting it. After the ring has been correctly fitted in the groove, fit the new element in the oil-filter body. Locate the body on the head and tighten the centre bolt.

Refill the sump to the correct level. Approximately 6¾ pints of oil (7½ pints after December 1964) will be required for this operation due to the extra oil contained in the oil filter. Start the engine and check for any external leaks or any leaks from the oil-filter body.

A ventilator is incorporated in the engine oil-filler cap and this should also be cleaned at this mileage. To do this wash the cap in petrol, and re-oil the gauze fitted in the cap. Shake off any surplus oil before refitting the cap.

Although it is normally only necessary to drain the engine oil and renew the filter element at 5,000 miles, this should be done earlier if it is thought that the oil has become excessively contaminated for any reason.

Flushing the Sump

Although it is normally not considered necessary to flush out the sump, it can be done at this period after draining the engine oil but before renewing the oil-filter element. If it is decided to flush out the sump, refit the sump drain plug and fill the engine to the 'FULL' mark on the dipstick with a flushing oil; under no circumstances use paraffin for this operation. Start up the engine and allow it to run for a few

minutes then drain off the flushing oil, renew the oil-filter element as described previously, and refill the sump to its correct level with new engine oil.

Removing the Oil Sump

If it is necessary to remove the oil sump in order to renew defective sump gaskets, the engine must be detached from its mountings and raised at the front approximately 2 in. At the same time, the starter motor must be removed. After the sump has been removed, the oil-pump inlet pipe and the gauze strainer can be detached, if necessary, by unscrewing the union nut from its location in the block.

24. CHANGING OIL-FILTER ELEMENT

The full-flow oil filter, mounted on an external rotor-type oil pump, should have its replaceable element changed every 5,000 miles.

The oil filter body and element can be detached after removing the centre bolt which is on top of the oil-pump body.

When renewing the element, always use a new rubber-sealing ring supplied with each replaceable element.

When fitting the rubber-ring in the filter head, locate it in the groove at four diametrically opposite points and then push it home.

Before refitting the sump, thoroughly clean off the old gaskets from the sump flange, locate the new gaskets on the flange, securing them with grease, and ensure that the tabs on the ends of the gaskets are correctly located in the grooves at the front and rear of the sump. Locate the cork packing-strips in the grooves by pushing each end securely into place so that it locks the tab on the sump gaskets and then compress the rest of the cork strip into location in the groove. Replace the sump, tightening the bolts securely and evenly and refill the engine with new oil.

Crankcase Ventilation Tube

To remove unwanted combustion products from the crankcase, a ventilation tube is mounted on the right-hand side of the cylinder block. The movement of the car causes a draught of air around the bottom of this tube and the vacuum so created draws oil fumes, etc. from the crankcase. Fresh air passes into the crankcase through the gauze filter in the oil-filler cap. No maintenance is called for on this, apart from cleaning the gauze in the oil-filler cap every 5,000 miles as described previously, although occasionally the security of the vent pipe should be checked.

Tightening Manifold Bolts

At the same time as the cylinder-head bolts are tightened, the inlet- and exhaust-manifold bolts should be checked for tightness. Also check the exhaust pipe to manifold joint, ensuring that the nuts are tight to prevent exhaust gases passing into the body of the vehicle.

VALVE-CLEARANCE ADJUSTMENT

To ensure the maximum engine performance,

25. SEQUENCE FOR TIGHTENING CYLINDER-HEAD BOLTS

The numbering indicates the sequence in which the cylinder-head bolts should be progressively tightened, in order to avoid distortion of the cylinder-head.

Where a torque spanner is available, the bolts should be finally tightened to a torque of 65–70 lb-ft; this will prevent the possibility of overtightening these bolts.

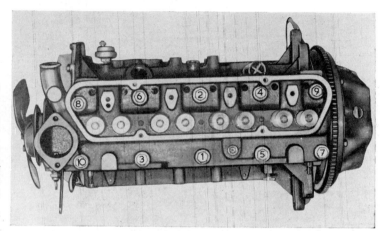

TIGHTENING CYLINDER-HEAD BOLTS

After the first 500 miles running on a new or reconditioned engine, or after the cylinder-head gasket has been renewed, the tightness of the cylinder-head bolts should be checked. It is important that these bolts are not over-tightened and to prevent this the manufacturers stipulate that the bolts should be tightened to a torque of 65–70 lb-ft. This is a measurement of the leverage of the spanner and the effort applied at the end of the spanner, that is, if a spanner with a leverage of one foot is used to tighten the bolt, the effort applied at the end of the lever should be 65–70 lb. Similarly, if the lever is two feet long, the effort would be $32\frac{1}{2}$–35 lb.

Remove the valve-rocker cover, after unscrewing the four bolts and spring washers securing it to the cylinder head and tighten the cylinder-head bolts to the specified torque in the order shown in Fig. 25. Tighten the bolts evenly to prevent distortion of the cylinder head.

the valve clearance, that is, the clearance between the end of the valve stem and the rocker with the push-rod in its lowest position, should be checked at the first 500-mile service and then every 5,000 miles. If these clearances are excessive, the engine will be noisy in operation and loss of power will result. On the other hand, if the clearances are too small, valve burning will occur.

This operation should be carried out with the engine hot. Remove the rocker cover and lift off the rocker-cover gasket. The overhead-valve gear will now be exposed and valves 1, 4, 5 and 8 (numbering from the front of the engine) are exhaust and numbers 2, 3, 6 and 7 are inlet valves. The engine must be rotated to carry out this operation and it is recommended that the spark plugs be removed and the engine turned by a suitable spanner on the end of the crankshaft-pulley-securing bolt.

Rotate the engine until numbers 1 and 6 valves are both open by an equal amount. When the valves are in this position, numbers 3 and

8 can be checked. Insert a feeler of the correct thickness between the valve stem and rocker and, if necessary, to adjust the clearance, slacken the adjusting-screw locknut on the opposite end of the valve rocker and adjust the screw as necessary. The clearance is correct when the feeler blade can be just withdrawn from between the rocker arm and valve stem. When the clearance is correct hold the adjusting screw and tighten the locknut.

Repeat this operation for all valves, setting

the inlet-valve clearance to 0·010 in. and the exhaust-valve clearance to 0·017 in. On G.T. models, these clearances should be 0·014 in. and 0·021 in. respectively. The table given below gives the easiest method of adjusting these valve clearances. Set the valves in the left-hand column, headed 'Valves Open' so that they are both equally open and adjust the clearances of the valves in the right-hand column.

Valves Open	Valves to Adjust
1 and 6	3 and 8
3 and 8	1 and 6
2 and 4	5 and 7
5 and 7	2 and 4

(Numbering from front of engine, 1, 4, 5 and 8 are exhaust valves and 2, 3, 6 and 7 are inlet valves.)

Fit a new valve rocker-cover gasket to the cylinder-head face, locate the rocker cover on the gasket and retain it in position with four bolts and lock washers.

EXCESSIVE OIL CONSUMPTION

It should be stressed that all engines will use some oil but if this is found to be excessive it may be due to either oil leaks from the engine or oil being burnt in the cylinders. It is advisable to keep the engine clean externally so that any oil leaks may be seen before they become excessive. If the leaks are from the rocker cover or sump flange, the gaskets should be renewed if the bolts are found to be securely tightened.

If oil is being burnt in the cylinders, this will

26. VALVE-CLEARANCE ADJUSTMENT

It is most important that there should be a clearance between the end of the valve stem and rocker when the push rod is at its lowest position.

The clearance, when the engine is hot, should be 0·010 in. for the inlet and 0·017 in. for the exhaust valves on standard engines. On the G.T. engine, the clearance (hot) should be 0·014 in. for inlet and 0·021 in. for exhaust valves.

The clearance is correct when a feeler gauge of the appropriate thickness can just be withdrawn from between the valve stem and rocker.

The clearance is adjusted by the screw after slackening the locknut. Retighten locknut after the correct gap is obtained.

Numbering from front of engine, the exhaust valves are 1, 4, 5, 8 and the inlet 2, 3, 6, 7.

be noticeable by the fact that the exhaust smoke will be blue in colour. To check for this, allow the engine to idle for a short period and then open the throttle, when, if oil is being burnt, a cloud of blue smoke will be seen coming from the exhaust pipe. This oil may be passing into the cylinders due either to worn valve guides or oil seals or worn pistons and rings, although the latter will not normally take place until a high mileage has been covered and at the same time will be accompanied by a loss in power and general poor performance of the engine. If oil is passing the pistons and rings this may, at the same time, give rise to excessive fumes from the crankcase.

Where oil consumption is due to worn pistons and rings, the only satisfactory cure is to have the engine completely overhauled and new pistons and rings fitted, after having the cylinders rebored.

Umbrella-type rubber oil seals are fitted to each valve stem and if oil is passing into the cylinders due to these being worn, they can be renewed. For their removal, see under 'Removing Valves'.

If at any time the oil-warning light remains permanently 'ON', or the oil-pressure gauge reading is very low, the engine should not be run, but a check made for this loss in oil pressure. Loss of oil pressure may be due to low oil level, stuck oil-pump relief valve or a very badly worn engine. The oil-pressure relief valve is incorporated in the oil pump mounted in the head of the filter body. If necessary, the oil pump can be removed from the engine after unscrewing the three bolts securing it to the cylinder block – the relief valve can be seen located in the pump-mounting flange. If this valve is free, the engine must be dismantled to check for the drop in oil pressure.

ENGINE FAULTS

The majority of engine faults can generally be traced to some defect in the fuel or ignition systems. Before deciding to check for any engine defect, the fuel and ignition systems should be thoroughly checked to ensure that everything is correct.

DECARBONIZING AND VALVE GRINDING

After high mileages, the valves and their seatings may become burnt so that they no longer make a good gas-tight joint and this may give rise to loss of power, difficult starting and, at the same time, may be noticeable by a spitting back in the carburetter or popping in the exhaust system. At the same time, excessive carbon deposits may have been built up on the cylinder head and pistons, which may also cause loss of power, pinking and possibly overheating.

If it is decided to decarbonize the engine and regrind the valves it will be necessary to have a valve-spring compressor, a blunt scraper and a valve-grinding tool fitted with a rubber suction cup. When the engine is decarbonized all the necessary gaskets should be replaced and these can be obtained as a special kit from any Ford Dealer.

Removing Cylinder Head

Drain the cooling system by opening the taps at the bottom of the radiator and on the left-hand side of the engine. It is important that the radiator cap be removed to allow the engine to drain completely. If the engine contains anti-freeze, the cooling water should be retained so that this can be put back into the cooling system afterwards.

To prevent possible damage to the electrical system, the battery should be disconnected. Disconnect the plug leads by pulling them off the plug terminals and unscrew the sparking plugs. Remove the air cleaner from the carburetter, unscrew the clips securing the radiator hose to the radiator and cylinder-head outlet and pull off the hose. Disconnect the lead from the temperature-gauge unit at the front of the cylinder head.

Remove the valve-rocker cover and then lift off the gasket. Disconnect the distributor vacuum pipe from the carburetter by pulling the rubber connection from the carburetter. Unscrew the petrol-pipe union from the carburetter and disconnect all throttle and choke connections. Disconnect the exhaust pipe from the manifold, unscrew the nuts and bolts securing the manifold to the cylinder head and pull off the manifold (removal of the G.T. exhaust manifold is mentioned below).

G.T. Models – On G.T. models, disconnect the hoses from the inlet manifold, unscrew the four bolts and flat washers securing the manifold to the cylinder head and pull off the manifold. The inlet manifold is aligned to the cylinder head by two locating rings fitted in Nos. 1 and 4 inlet ports; take care not to lose or damage these when removing the manifold.

The exhaust manifold is still retained to the cylinder head by a bolt through the flange of Nos. 1 and 4 pipes; remove these bolts and it can be moved away from the engine. Where the exhaust manifold is to be removed, unscrew the clamp-bolt nuts and detach the two semi-circular clamps securing the manifold outlet pipe to the silencer inlet pipe.

All Models – Unscrew the rocker-shaft securing bolts and lift off the rocker shaft. The push-rods can now be lifted out of the cylinder block; these should be numbered and retained in their correct location. Unscrew the cylinder-head bolts in the reverse order to the tightening sequence shown in Fig. 25, and the cylinder head can now be lifted off. If the head is found to be tight do not try to separate it from the block by forcing a screwdriver or similar tool in between the two faces. To free a tight cylinder head, tap the side of the head with a wooden mallet.

Removing Valves

Once the cylinder head has been detached, the valves can now be removed. Using a valve-spring compressor, compress the spring and remove the collets located at the end of the valve stem. Release the compressor and the spring and its retainer can now be pulled off. An umbrella-type rubber seal is fitted to the valve stem; pull off this seal and remove the valve from its valve guide. The valves should be retained in their correct position. Do not stamp or punch the heads of the valves for identification purposes, but place them in a suitably numbered board to identify them for reassembly. Dismantle all valves in this manner and the cylinder head can now be decarbonized.

Removing Carbon

Thoroughly scrape all carbon from the cylinder head and from the valve ports. After the carbon has been removed, thoroughly wash the cylinder head with paraffin to make sure all traces of carbon are washed off. This is to prevent carbon reaching the working parts on reassembly and causing consequential damage.

The carbon on the piston crowns can now be removed. Before doing this, smear grease around the top of each cylinder bore, then turn the crankshaft so that two pistons are at the top of their respective bores. Insert rag into the other two cylinders to prevent carbon falling into the bores and scrape off all the carbon from the piston crown. Take care when doing this that the piston crown is not scored or damaged in any way. Either an old screwdriver or wood chisel with their edges dulled or blunt will serve as a scraping tool.

After the first pair of pistons have been decarbonized, remove the rag from the cylinder bores and proceed to deal with the other pair of pistons by turning the crankshaft a half revolution to bring them to the top of their stroke. Do not forget to place the rag in the cylinder bores of the cleaned pistons before scraping the carbon from the crown of the second pair of pistons.

Grinding-in Exhaust Valves

After scraping all carbon from the valve heads and stems, the exhaust valves should be ground into their seatings to ensure a good gas-tight joint, so preventing loss of power. The inlet valves have an aluminized finish on their seats and these should never be ground in or this coating will be destroyed. If the seats are burnt or pitted, new valves must be fitted. The inlet-valve seats in the cylinder head must be refaced if they are damaged; this operation is carried out by using a slave inlet valve for lapping purposes.

To grind in the exhaust valves (or to recondition the inlet-valve seats in the cylinder head), smear a small quantity of grinding paste on the taper seat on the valve head and fit the valve in its own valve guide. Fit the rubber-suction valve grinder to the head of the valve and rotate the valve backwards and forwards on its seat. At the same time as the valve is rotated on its seat it should be lifted occasionally to prevent grooving of the valve seat. Withdraw the valve from its seat, wipe off all grinding paste from the valve and cylinder head and check the condition of the seat.

This grinding operation should be continued until a matt grey surface is obtained all round the seat on the valve head and in the cylinder head. Repeat this operation for all valves. After the valves have been ground-in, thoroughly wash all traces of grinding paste from the valves and cylinder head.

Reassembling Cylinder Head

The cylinder head can now be reassembled as follows. Insert the valves in their own valve guides, placing a few drops of oil on each valve stem before it is inserted. Fit new oil seals to the valve stems and locate the spring on the seating in the cylinder head. Fit the spring retainer at the top end of the spring and compress the spring by means of the valve-spring compressor. Fit the two tapered collets on to the end of the valve stem with their smaller diameter towards the valve spring and make sure they are located in the valve-stem groove. Release the valve-spring compressor gradually so that the collets will be held by the spring retainer. Repeat this for all valves.

Before refitting the cylinder head ensure that the faces of the cylinder head and cylinder block are thoroughly clean. Wipe the cylinder bores and squirt a few drops of oil into each cylinder before refitting the head. Locate the new cylinder-head gasket on the block face; the gasket is marked 'TOP' and must only be fitted this way up. The outer edges of the gasket should be smeared with a good jointing compound before fitting. It is advisable to use two locating studs screwed into diagonally opposite corners to locate the gasket. These studs can be made by sawing the heads off two spare cylinder-head bolts. Refit the cylinder head, locating it on the studs and enter all the cylinder-head bolts.

The cylinder-head bolts can now be tightened in the sequence shown in Fig. 25. Do not tighten the bolts excessively to begin with, but tighten each one a little at a time and in the order shown, finally tightening them to the correct torque of 65–70 lb-ft. Refit the push-rods in their correct locations, making sure that the ball end at the bottom of the rod is seating correctly in the tappet. Refit the rocker shaft, again making sure that the upper ends of the push-rods are located correctly on the rocker-arm adjusting screws. Fit and tighten the rocker-shaft bolts. Adjust the valve clearances as described previously – these will have to be re-checked after the engine has warmed up. Refit the inlet and exhaust manifold using a new gasket.

G.T. Models – On G.T. cars locate the inlet-manifold locating rings in Nos. 1 and 4 induction ports in the cylinder head and fit the gasket locating it on these rings. Fit the exhaust manifold, securing it with two bolts and flat washers through the front and rear flanges, then fit the inlet manifold and the other bolts and flat washers to retain both manifolds to the cylinder head.

All Models – Reconnect the choke and throttle controls and fit the distributor vacuum pipe and petrol pipe to the carburetter. Refit the radiator rubber hose and the hoses to the inlet manifold on G.T. cars, tightening the clamps securely. Locate a new valve-rocker cover gasket on the cylinder head and refit the valve-rocker cover. Reconnect the temperature-gauge lead to the unit in the cylinder head. Reconnect the exhaust pipe to the manifold, tightening the nuts securely. Refit the spark plugs, making sure that each one has a copper gasket fitted to it. Tighten the plugs and reconnect the plug leads. Reconnect the battery and refill the cooling system.

Start up the engine and allow it to warm up to its normal working temperature. Then re-check the cylinder-head bolt tightness and valve clearances. These should again be checked after the car has run 500 miles.

It is advisable when the engine is decarbonized that, at the same time, the fuel and ignition systems are overhauled, and full details of these are given in the appropriate chapters.

RUNNING-IN A NEW OR RECONDITIONED ENGINE

With a new or reconditioned engine, it is recommended that for the first 500 miles, the following speeds should not be exceeded: top gear 45 m.p.h.; third gear 30 m.p.h.; second gear 20 m.p.h.; and first gear 10 m.p.h. These speeds should not be sustained for long periods but occasional short bursts at these speeds will help the engine to run in. The engine should not be allowed to labour hard on a hill – change to a lower gear but, at the same time, the change down should not be made too early to avoid the engine racing in the intermediate gears. The engine should not be allowed to idle for long periods, particularly when starting from cold, but rather be started up and the car driven away immediately.

As the engine settles down, it may be found that, to ensure the optimum performance, the ignition and the carburetter will need slight adjustment.

With a new or reconditioned engine, it may be found that the oil consumption does not settle down to a steady figure until well past the end of the running-in period. This is due to the type of piston rings fitted, which take longer to bed in than the other working components.

c

Chapter 5

FUEL SYSTEM

AN 8-gallon-capacity tank is mounted at the rear of the car under the luggage-boot floor. A mechanical fuel pump, operated by the engine camshaft, draws fuel from the tank to supply a downdraught carburetter. Engines fitted with the high-compression cylinder head should only be operated on premium-grade fuel, although the low-compression engine will operate satisfactorily on regular-grade fuel.

Little maintenance is called for on the fuel system, apart from keeping the fuel clean and checking for any fuel leaks. Occasionally check all fuel connections from the tank to pump and the pump to carburetter for any leaks. At the first 500-mile service and every 5,000 miles, the filter incorporated in the lift pump should be cleaned to prevent dirt being passed to the float chamber. The air cleaner should be cleaned every 5,000 miles, or more frequently under dusty conditions.

The fuel tank is fitted with a non-vented-type filler cap and if at any time this has to be replaced, only this type should be used. If a vented cap is fitted it will allow fuel spillage on inclines. The fuel tank is vented to atmosphere by an inverted V-shaped pipe connected to the filler neck and passing back through the boot floor.

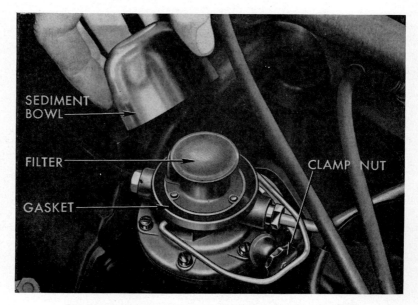

27. FUEL-PUMP SEDIMENT BOWL AND FILTER

The filter screen and sediment chamber should be cleaned every 5,000 miles, after removing the sediment-bowl secured by a clamp nut. Clean any sediment from the pump chamber and wash the filter in petrol.

When replacing the bowl, check that the gasket is in good condition – if in doubt, renew it.

FUEL PUMP

The mechanical-type fuel pump is bolted on the right-hand rear of the cylinder block and is operated by the engine camshaft. The pump is entirely automatic in action and requires little maintenance, apart from cleaning the filter screen regularly and removing sediment from the pump chamber.

The fuel-pump screen and sediment chamber should be cleaned every 5,000 miles. To do this unscrew the clamp on top of the bowl, lift off the bowl and detach the filter screen. Any sediment which may have collected in the pump chamber can now be washed out. Also wash the filter screen in petrol, making sure all particles of dirt are removed, and refit the screen to the pump. Check that the gasket is in good condition or, fit a new gasket to the pump, and refit the bowl to the pump body, tightening the retaining clamp securely.

Checking Fuel Pump

If at any time it is thought that the fuel pump is not supplying fuel, a simple check on its delivery can be made by disconnecting the outlet pipe from the fuel pump and operating the engine on the starter motor. As the fuel pump operates, a distinct spurt of petrol should be seen from the outlet union. If there is no delivery of fuel from the pump, first check the supply to the pump for blockage before deciding that the pump is faulty. To do this disconnect the inlet pipe from the pump and blow through the pipe to the fuel tank. A blocked fuel-tank vent pipe will also cause a restriction in the fuel supply; some indication of this may be given by air being drawn into the tank when the filler cap is released. If the supply pipe from the fuel tank to pump and the vent pipe are clear, check the fuel-pump vacuum by holding a finger over the pump inlet union and again cranking the engine with the starter motor. If the pump is operating satisfactorily a depression should be felt, if there is no depression, the fuel pump is faulty. If there is a depression on the pump it may be that there is an air leak on the fuel inlet line and a check should be made for this.

CARBURETTER

Two types of carburetter are used on these models, according to the type of engine fitted: Standard and De Luxe models have a single-venturi downdraught Zenith 33 VN2 carburetter, whilst the G.T. models have a twin-choke dual downdraught Weber 28/36 DCD instrument; both types incorporate an accelerator pump. The general maintenance is similar in both cases and is covered below, peculiarities of each type being dealt with separately.

Occasionally, the security of the carburetter-to-manifold retaining nuts should be checked, but they must not be overtightened, otherwise the carburetter flange may distort, so causing air leaks, giving loss of power and possible overheating. A spanner with a leverage of not more than 3 in. should be used when checking these nuts. At the same time a check can be made on the float-chamber securing screws; again these should not be overtightened.

Whenever the carburetter is checked for security, inspect the rubber pipe connecting the distributor vacuum pipe to the carburetter to see that this is not perished or cracked, so allowing air leaks, which will give a weak mixture and also affect the ignition timing of the engine.

The carburetter ball joints and accelerator cross linkage secured to the bulkhead should be lubricated with a few drops of engine oil occasionally to prevent sticking and to give smooth operation of the controls.

Slow-running Adjustment

Two controls are provided on the carburetter to adjust the engine slow running. These are the hexagon-headed slow-running adjustment screw which controls the engine speed and the knurled volume-control screw which controls the amount of mixture drawn into the engine under these conditions.

This adjustment should only be carried out with the engine at normal working temperature. To do this first make sure that the air cleaner is clean, then screw in the slow-running adjustment screw until the engine runs at a fast-idling speed. Unscrew the volume-control screw until the engine starts to roll or hunt, then slowly screw in the volume-control screw until the engine runs evenly. When the engine

 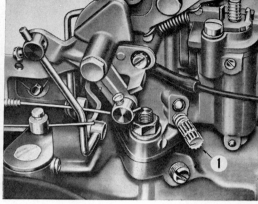

1. Slow-running adjustment screw.   1. Volume-control screw.

28. SLOW-RUNNING ADJUSTMENT – ZENITH 33 VN2 CARBURETTER

The slow-running adjustment is carried out as follows with the engine at working temperature.
(A) Set slow-running adjustment (throttle) screw until engine runs at a fast idling speed.
(B) Unscrew volume-control screw until engine begins to hunt.
(C) Screw it in again gradually until hunting disappears and engine idles smoothly.
(D) If engine speed has risen, then reset slow-running screw to get a normal idling speed.
(E) This may cause a slight resumption of hunting. If so, gently screw in volume-control screw until idling is perfect.
Under no circumstances should the volume-control screw be screwed hard home.

runs evenly, screw out the slow-running adjustment screw to get a normal idling speed. This adjustment may cause the engine to start hunting. If so, screw in the volume-control screw until the engine runs evenly. When carrying out this adjustment, the volume-control screw should only be moved a small amount at a time and the engine allowed to settle down at each fresh setting before making a further adjustment.

On the G.T. models, the idling speed should be set to 650 r.p.m. on the tachometer; do not set it below this speed or the engine will idle roughly due to its high-compression ratio.

Choke Control

If at any time the choke control has been disconnected from the carburetter, care should be taken when reconnecting it that when the lever on the carburetter is in the full 'OFF' position (fully forward), there is approximately $\frac{1}{8}$ in. gap between the choke-control knob and the dash panel. If this precaution is not observed, slight movement of the engine may pull the choke into the 'ON' position when running.

Zenith Carburetter (Standard Engine)

A single-venturi downdraught Zenith carburetter is fitted to Standard engines. This has a piston-type accelerator pump and all jets are internal. The jets are located in the float chamber which can be detached after unscrewing the two bolts holding it to the body of the carburetter. The accelerator-pump jet is screwed into the front face of the float chamber; all other jets are fitted in the emulsion block located in the float chamber and secured to the front face by two screws. Remove the screws, and lift out the block to obtain access to the jets. A strangler flap valve is fitted for starting.

The accelerator-pump stroke is variable, the length of stroke being controlled by a stop around the piston-operating rod in the float-chamber cover. This stop has two lugs on it, one being longer than the other, which contact the piston-operating lever. In summer, the stop should be set with the long lug under the lever; this will give a short stroke to the accelerator pump. Under cold conditions it may be necessary to rotate the stop half a turn so that the short lug is below the lever, so permitting a longer stroke on the accelerator pump. To turn the stop, it must be lifted clear of the float-chamber cover against the tension of the light coil spring, as it is located in the cover by two flats machined on the sides. After adjusting the stop, make sure it is fully seated in the cover.

Weber Carburetter (G.T. Engine)

This is a dual-barrel instrument, with a double venturi in each barrel. Each barrel is a separate carburetter having its own jets and throttle plate and has a double venturi or choke

29. PAPER ELEMENT AND OIL-WETTED GAUZE AIR CLEANERS

The filtering element of both types of cleaner should receive attention every 5,000 and the paper-type element be renewed every 15,000 miles.

After removing the gauze-type element, wash it in petrol and allow to dry. Then dip the element in engine oil, shake out the excess oil and refit it to the cleaner body.

With a paper-type element, shake off the dust after removing it from the body and then refit it after cleaning the body.

tube fitted to give good fuel emulsification. The throttle plates are interconnected, the linkage being set so that at small throttle openings or when idling, fuel is supplied by the primary barrel only. As the primary throttle is opened further, the secondary throttle starts to open, bringing the secondary barrel of the carburetter into operation.

A piston-type accelerator pump is fitted, this discharging into the primary barrel only; the pump stroke is non-adjustable. The starting device is itself a separate carburetter and gives a progressively rich mixture as the choke control is pulled out.

A cast-aluminium four-branch inlet manifold is fitted to G.T. engines and is heated by the engine coolant to ensure full-fuel vaporization under normal operating conditions. Water is taken from the front of the cylinder head to the front of the manifold. From the rear of the manifold, the water passes back to the water pump or, if a heater is fitted, to a T-connection in the return pipe from the heater to the water

pump. The manifold is aligned to the cylinder head by two tubular dowels, fitted in Nos. 1 and 4 manifold ports. If the manifold is removed at any time, take care not to lose these dowels.

AIR CLEANER

Two types of air cleaner are fitted, these being either an oil-wetted gauze or a paper-element type. Both types should be cleaned every 5,000 miles and the paper-element type renewed every 15,000 miles.

To remove both types of cleaner element, detach the bolt retaining the top cover to the air-cleaner body, lift off the cover and take out the element. If it is the gauze type, wash the element in petrol and, when dry, dip it in engine oil, shake off the excess oil and refit it after cleaning the body of the cleaner unit. Where a paper element is fitted, remove this carefully from the body, shake off the dust and replace it after cleaning the body.

When renewing the paper element every 15,000 miles, also fit a new sealing ring in the cover and body of the cleaner unit.

FUEL-SYSTEM FAULTS

Fuel-system faults can be classified under the two broad headings of: (a) Rich Mixture and (b) Weak Mixture. The carburetter has been designed to supply the correct mixture strength of fuel and air under all conditions. If too much fuel or too little air is supplied, this gives rise to rich mixture; conversely, too little fuel or too much air will cause a weak mixture.

FUEL-SYSTEM CHECK

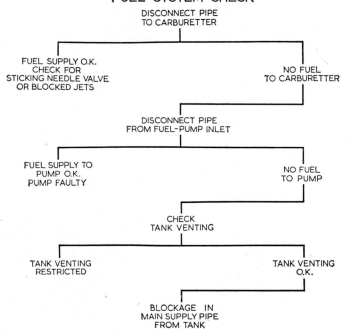

Causes of Rich Mixture

1. Blocked air cleaner
2. Enlarged fuel jets
3. Excessively high float-chamber level
4. Incorrectly adjusted choke control
5. Sticking carburetter needle valve
6. High fuel-pump pressure
7. Restricted air-correction jets

Causes of Weak Mixture

1. Air leaks anywhere on the induction system
2. Enlarged air-correction jets
3. Restricted petrol jets
4. Low float-chamber level
5. Low fuel-pump pressure

Effects of Rich Mixture

1. Loss of power
2. Dirty exhaust
3. Soft sooty deposit on spark plugs
4. Heavy fuel consumption
5. Backfiring in exhaust system

Effects of Weak Mixture

1. Loss of power
2. Difficult starting
3. Overheating
4. Spitting back in carburetter
5. Hard white deposit on spark-plug points

The above are the faults which may arise with the fuel system, but these will normally be restricted to fuel starvation due to blocked jets or restricted fuel-pump delivery. These can be easily isolated. For example, if the engine will start using the choke control, but stops immediately it is pushed in, or alternatively, will run at high speeds but will not idle, both these faults indicate that the idling-petrol jet is restricted. Similarly, if the engine will start and idle but will not run at high speeds, this indicates that the main jet is restricted. Remove the jet affected and blow through this to clear any blockage.

If the engine will not start, check the fuel supply to the carburetter by slackening the petrol pipe to carburetter union and turning the engine on the starter motor. If the fuel supply is correct, a good spurt of petrol will be seen from the end of the pipe. If there is no fuel at the end of the pipe, check the delivery from the pump and the fuel supply to the pump, as outlined previously in this chapter. If petrol is supplied at the end of the pipe, check that this is passing to the float chamber by slackening one of the jets in the float chamber side (on G.T. models) when fuel should run out from the float chamber.

Where fuel is not passing to the float chamber, this can be due to the needle valve in the float-chamber cover being stuck on its seating. To rectify this, remove the air cleaner, disconnect the fuel pipe from the float-chamber cover and lift off the cover after unscrewing the bolts and spring washers which secure it to the body. The needle valve will be seen screwed into the top of the float-chamber cover and the valve spindle should move quite freely in its housing. If the valve spindle is sticking, wash the assembly in petrol, turning the valve on its seat to remove any gum which may be present. Once the valve moves freely, refit the cover, reconnect the fuel pipe and refit the air cleaner.

On the Zenith carburetter, all jets are internal and the float chamber must be removed to check fuel flow. Alternatively, remove the air cleaner and operate the throttle lever and a jet of fuel should be seen discharged into the choke tube. If no fuel is present, the needle valve screwed into the face of the float-chamber cover may be sticking. Unscrew the valve after removing the float chamber, taking care not to lose the washers fitted to it and wash the valve in petrol to free it.

If the air cleaner is not maintained correctly, it will become restricted, so restricting the air supply to the engine, causing a rich mixture. Under dusty conditions, the air cleaner should be cleaned more frequently than the normal 5,000-mile period.

Air Leaks in the Induction System

The main cause of a weak mixture which will generally give rise to difficult starting, over-heating, loss of power and spitting back in the carburetter, are air leaks, anywhere in the induction system. These air leaks can generally be traced to faulty carburetter-flange gaskets or manifold gaskets. To check these gaskets, allow the engine to idle and squirt a few drops of oil around the flange joint and similarly around the manifold joint; if either or both joints are faulty, the oil will be seen to be drawn into the manifold. At the same time, the exhaust smoke will turn into a light blue colour. Where air leaks are present, the gaskets should be renewed as necessary.

At the same time, check the distributor-vacuum pipe connection to the carburetter to see that the rubber pipe is not perished, as this again will give air leaks in addition to causing incorrect ignition timing.

Fault-finding Chart

The accompanying fault-finding chart gives the points to check on the fuel system when investigating any erratic engine operation. It is suggested that the engine ignition system be checked thoroughly before checking the fuel system, as the majority of engine faults are mainly due to ignition causes.

Chapter 6

COOLING SYSTEM

THE cooling system of the Consul Corsair is a pressurized thermo-syphon type with water pump assistance, the pump being bolted to the front face of the cylinder block.

A thermostat is fitted in the cylinder-head water outlet to restrict water circulation during the warming-up period. The thermostat is a temperature-controlled valve which starts to open between 83° C. (181° F.) and 88° C. (190° F.) and is fully open at 99° C. (210° F.). When the thermostat is closed, the water is trapped in the cylinder head and cylinder block and, consequently, the engine reaches its normal working temperature more quickly than if the whole volume of cooling water were circulating round the system. As the water temperature reaches the opening temperature of the thermo-

stat, the thermostat opens, allowing the water to circulate through the radiator.

The circulation of water is from the bottom tank of the radiator to the water pump, where it is passed into the cylinder block, round the cylinder-head combustion chambers, past the thermostat to the top tank of the radiator. Air passing across the radiator cools the water and the cooled water falls to the bottom of the radiator passing up to the water pump and again round the system.

On G.T. models, the inlet manifold is heated by the engine coolant to ensure full fuel vaporization – water from the cylinder head enters the front of the manifold and is returned to the water pump from the rear of the manifold.

The cooling system holds approximately 11

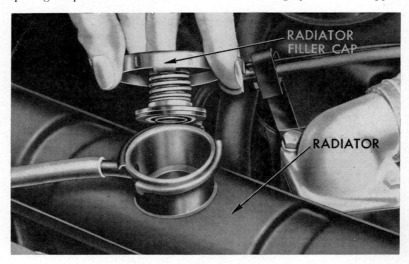

30. RADIATOR FILLER CAP

The radiator filler cap, which contains a pressurized valve, should never be removed while the engine is running. To do so invites the risk of severe scalding through the sudden ejection of near-boiling water.

When removing the cap with the engine still hot, turn it anti-clockwise very slowly.

pints of water; if a heater is fitted this is increased to 13 pints.

COOLING-SYSTEM MAINTENANCE

Little maintenance is called for in the cooling system. Where possible only soft water should be used. Occasionally inspect all hose connections to make sure they are not leaking and check the hoses for external cracking. Where there are signs of cracking, the hoses should be renewed. The system should be flushed out approximately twice each year and the tension of the fan belt should be checked every 5,000 miles.

Where an engine overheats, it should be remembered that the main causes of this are either a weak fuel mixture or incorrect ignition timing, and checks for these should be made. When the cooling system is suspected, first test the fan-belt tension to ensure that it is not slipping, so preventing the fan and water pump from turning. If the tension of the belt is correct, check the thermostat to see whether it is opening correctly.

Similarly, if the engine does not reach normal working temperature, examine the thermostat to ensure that it has not stuck in the wide-open position.

RADIATOR PRESSURE CAP

A pressurized radiator-filler cap (10 lb/sq. in.) is fitted to the top tank of the radiator. The effect of using a pressurized cap is to increase the boiling point of the cooling water to approximately 107° C. An internal-combustion engine becomes more efficient as its temperature increases and, provided the cooling water is not actually boiling, the hotter the water the more efficient the engine. Should the cooling-water temperature exceed the higher boiling point, the pressure build-up forces the pressure-release valve, attached to the radiator cap, off its seat and allows the water to pass through the radiator overflow pipe to atmosphere.

As the engine cools down, an atmospheric (vacuum-release) valve in the centre of the pressure-release valve is drawn off its seat. This allows air to enter the cooling system through the overflow pipe to prevent a partial vacuum being formed in the system.

Care should be taken when removing this type of radiator cap with a hot engine. Although the water may not be boiling its temperature may be above normal boiling point and immediately the cap is released, the pressure on the cooling water is also released, which may cause boiling and personal injury. When removing the cap, turn it anti-clockwise very slowly if the engine is hot.

FILLING COOLING SYSTEM

When filling the cooling system with water, do not fill the radiator right to the base of the filler neck but rather approximately 1 in. below this point. This will allow for expansion of the cooling water as it becomes hot. If the radiator is filled to the base of the filler neck, as the water expands the pressure cap will be lifted off its seat and the water lost through the overflow pipe. If the cooling system contains anti-freeze, and the radiator is regularly filled to this level, due to the loss of coolant through the overflow pipe the anti-freeze solution will be gradually diluted, possibly to the danger level.

If the engine has overheated, due to loss of coolant, allow it to cool down before refilling the radiator. Adding cold water to an overheated engine may cause cracking or distortion of the cylinder head, at the same time localized boiling may occur as the water is added, which could scald you.

FAN-BELT ADJUSTMENT

A two-blade 11 in.-diameter fan is bolted to the water-pump shaft and is driven in tandem with the generator by a vee-belt from the crankshaft pulley. The fan-belt tension should be checked every 5,000 miles. If the tension is too tight it will cause wear on the belt and possible damage to the water pump and generator bearings. Where the belt is too slack, slip will occur causing belt wear, possible overheating and erratic charging of the generator. To check the fan-belt tension, push and pull it at a point half-way between the generator and fan pulleys; the total free movement should be $\frac{1}{2}$ in. If the free movement is more than this, slacken the two bolts securing the generator to the mounting brackets on the cylinder block, slacken the top bolt on the generator-adjusting strap and swivel the generator on its mountings until the correct fan-belt tension is obtained. Tighten the adjusting-strap bolt and the generator mounting-bracket bolts.

The water pump shaft is mounted on a sealed bearing and no lubrication of the pump is required. Occasionally inspect under the pump housing for any signs of water leaks; where leaks are present, it indicates that the water-pump seal is faulty and must be renewed. Special tools are required to carry out this operation and it should be done by your Ford Dealer.

DRAINING AND FLUSHING COOLING SYSTEM

Two drain points are incorporated in the cooling system; a plug at the base of the radiator and a tap on the left-hand side of the cylinder block. To drain the system, release the radiator pressure cap, unscrew the plug and open the tap. If water does not drain from these points, probe them with a piece of wire to remove any obstructions. Similarly, after the

water has stopped running, again probe to make sure that the system is completely drained and that the drain points have not become obstructed.

It is recommended that the cooling system be drained and flushed out twice a year and a convenient time for doing this is before filling the system with anti-freeze and after draining off the anti-freeze solution at the end of winter. To do this, drain the system and, leaving both points open use a hose to run water into the top tank and so flush out any dirt in the system.

Many proprietary solutions can be obtained

31. FAN-BELT ADJUSTMENT

It is important that the tension of the fan belt is correctly maintained, and this should be checked every 5,000 miles and adjusted where necessary.

The tension is correct when the total free movement of the belt is $\frac{1}{2}$ in. measured at a point mid-way between the generator and fan pulleys.

To adjust the $\frac{1}{2}$-in. free movement of the fan belt, loosen the two generator-mounting bolts, one at the front and one at the rear, and slacken the adjustment locking bolt located in the slotted arm.

Swivel the generator on its mountings until the correct fan-belt tension is obtained. Then tighten the adjustment locking bolt and the two generator-mounting bolts.

which can be put into the cooling water to help flush out any deposits from the system.

ANTI-FREEZE SOLUTION

If an anti-freeze solution is used in the winter months, use only a good grade of anti-freeze as these contain inhibitors which prevent excessive rust formation or corrosion of the cooling system. Before filling the system with anti-freeze, flush out the whole cooling system. Mix the anti-freeze solution with cooling water before pouring the mixture into the radiator. One and a quarter pints of anti-freeze will give protection down to a temperature of approximately minus 8° C. (17° F.). In winter do not top up the radiator with water but use an anti-freeze solution, to prevent the solution in the cooling system becoming diluted, possibly to the danger point.

TEMPERATURE GAUGE

A water-temperature gauge is fitted in the instrument panel, controlled by a sender unit fitted in the cylinder head. Under normal operating conditions, the gauge needle should lie either in the sector marked 'H' or in the top end of the 'N' sector. Provided that the water is not actually boiling, the higher the temperature the more efficient the engine. If the gauge needle does not rise far into the 'N' sector, it may be that the thermostat is stuck open.

TESTING THERMOSTAT

To check the operation of the thermostat first remove it as follows. Drain the water from the cooling system, slacken the two clamps securing the top hose to the radiator and cylinder head and remove the hose. Unscrew the two bolts securing the water outlet to the cylinder head and lift out the thermostat. The operation of the thermostat can be checked by putting it in a container of water which is then gradually heated. With a thermometer check the temperature of the water at which the thermostat opens.

Where an engine does not reach its normal working temperature, it will usually indicate that the thermostat is stuck open and this will be visible immediately the thermostat is removed.

When replacing or renewing a faulty thermostat, fit a new gasket on to the water-outlet adaptor and secure this to the cylinder head with two bolts and spring washers. Refit the radiator hose, tighten the clamps and refill the cooling system with water. If anti-freeze is being used this, of course, must be retained and put back in the cooling system.

CHECKING FOR FAULTY CYLINDER-HEAD GASKET

If cooling water is being lost from the engine and there are no external leaks from radiator hoses, clips, etc., this may be due to a faulty cylinder-head gasket allowing cylinder pressure to force the cooling water out of the system. A check for this can be made by allowing the engine to run to its normal working temperature, removing the radiator cap and opening and closing the throttle. Any gas leaks from the gasket will cause bubbles in the cooling-water system. Take care not to confuse the normal agitation of the water due to the operation of the water pump with this condition. If this symptom is found, the cylinder-head gasket must be renewed.

Slight external seepage from the gasket can be often cured by the use of an anti-leak capsule, obtainable from any Ford Dealer. These capsules help seal any slight water leaks and, at the same time, act as a corrosion inhibitor and so help to keep the cooling system as a whole clean.

HEATER UNIT

The heater unit, when fitted, is bolted to the rear bulkhead of the engine compartment, and water from the cooling system passes through a radiator in the heater unit and back to the engine. Air blowing through the heater draws heat from the radiator before passing into the car. The water supply to the heater can be turned off if necessary by means of a tap on the left-hand side of the cylinder head. To do this, turn the shank of the tap with a spanner so that the line on the square end of the shank is at right angles to the outlet of the tap. The radiator of the heater is not drained when the engine cooling system is drained, so that anti-freeze should be used in winter months to prevent possible damage to this unit.

RADIATOR BLIND

Longer engine life and better fuel consumption can be obtained by running the engine as near its normal working temperature as possible; the use of a radiator blind, particularly in winter months, will help the engine to maintain its normal temperature and so help in prolonging engine life. In addition this will, of course, give an improved interior heater performance.

Chapter 7

IGNITION SYSTEM

THE ignition system has to transform the low-tension battery voltage to a high-tension voltage sufficient to jump the spark-plug gap under the high-compression pressures in the cylinders. The ignition system comprises two circuits: (1) The low-tension circuit, comprising the battery, ignition switch, low-tension winding of the ignition coil, contact-breaker points and condenser; (2) the high-tension circuit comprising the high-tension windings of the ignition coil, rotor, distributor cap and spark plugs – all these components are located on the right-hand side of the engine.

The high-tension current is induced in the coil through the interruption of the primary circuit by the contact-breaker points, and is distributed to the spark plugs in the correct firing order by the rotor and distributor cap.

The contact-breaker points are purely a mechanical switch opened by a four-lobe cam mounted on the distributor shaft. The rotor is located on top of the distributor cam and as the rotor rotates it lines up with the four segments in the cap, to which the spark-plug leads are connected. The condenser is fitted in parallel with the contact-breaker points and eliminates sparking at the points as they are opened, so helping to produce a good high-tension voltage. Any defect in the condenser will result in poor or no high-tension spark, thus causing difficult starting and misfiring or complete failure of ignition.

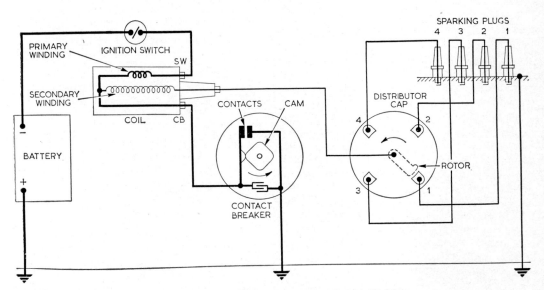

32. IGNITION-SYSTEM CIRCUIT DIAGRAM

The diagram shows the two circuits in the system – the primary (or low-tension) circuit and the secondary (or high-tension) circuit. The low-tension circuit is indicated by the thicker line. Note the 1243 firing order of the sparking plugs.

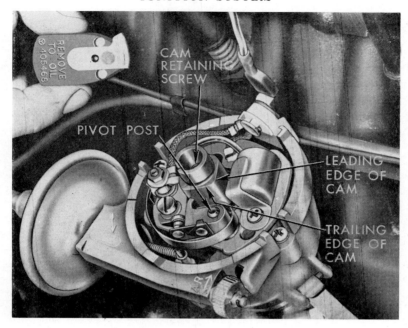

33. DISTRIBUTOR LUBRICATION

The distributor should be lubricated every 5,000 miles as follows:
Remove the distributor cap, secured by two spring clips and lift off the rotor.
Apply one or two drops of engine oil to the head of the cam-retaining screw. This oil will lubricate the distributor shaft and bearings.
Apply a thin smear of petroleum jelly to the distributor cam and a drop of oil to the pivot of the contact lever. Also lubricate the governor weights with a few drops of engine oil through the aperture in the contact-breaker plate.

The majority of vehicle failures on the road are due to ignition faults and consequently it is important that the ignition system is maintained in a serviceable condition. The heart of the ignition system, as with all car electrical systems, is the battery; if the battery is neglected, only poor performance of any electrical system will result. It is important, therefore, that the battery and its connections are maintained in a good condition. Full details of battery maintenance are given in Chapter 15.

To ensure maximum engine performance under all conditions, it is necessary to vary the ignition timing, that is, the point at which the spark occurs at the spark-plug points. This is done in two ways, firstly, by centrifugal weights in the distributor body, which vary the timing with engine speed. The second system is by means of a vacuum unit connected to the contact-breaker plate, on which the points are mounted and to a tapping in the throttle barrel of the carburetter, so that any variations in throttle vacuum are transmitted to the vacuum unit. The ignition timing is, therefore, adjusted according to engine load, being advanced when the vacuum is high due to a high air speed through the throttle barrel and retarded as the vacuum is reduced by a lower air speed through the throttle barrel. A knurled nut is fitted to the vacuum-unit advance spindle and this nut can be rotated to vary the ignition timing if necessary. Full details of this adjustment will be given later in this chapter.

MAINTENANCE SCHEDULE

Weekly Attention

Check the level of the electrolyte in the battery, check the cleanliness and tightness of the battery terminals.

Full details on battery maintenance are given in Chapter 15.

After First 500 Miles

Check and, if necessary, adjust the contact-breaker point gap.

Every 5,000 Miles

1. Lubricate the distributor.
2. Check condition of contact-breaker points and adjust gap if necessary.
3. Remove and clean spark plugs.

(The method of carrying out these maintenance attentions is given below.)

Distributor Lubrication

Release the spring clips securing the distributor cap in position and lift off the cap. This will expose the rotor on the end of the distributor drive shaft. Pull the rotor off the shaft and apply one or two drops of engine oil to the screw which can be seen in the centre of the shaft. This oil will lubricate the shaft so that the cam is free to move on it under the action of the automatic-advance weights. At the same time, the weights should be lubricated with a few drops of engine oil through the hole in the contact-breaker plate; also lubricate the moving contact-breaker pivot post with a drop of engine oil. The cam itself should be lubricated by a thin smear of petroleum jelly applied to the face of the cam. Do not over-lubricate any part of the distributor or lubricant may get on to the contact-breaker points, causing a poor spark or no spark at all.

Refit the rotor, taking care to push it right home on the spindle, then replace the cap, making sure that the spring clips retain it securely.

Adjusting Contact-breaker Points Gap

The contact-breaker point gap should be 0·014 to 0·016 in. when the points are fully open. To check this gap, remove the distributor cap and lift off the rotor. Rotate the crankshaft until the fibre heel on the moving point is on the high point of one of the cam lobes. With the points in this position, push the moving point as far open as possible and inspect the condition of the contact faces of the points. If these faces are dirty or pitted, the contact-breaker points should be removed and refaced. If the points

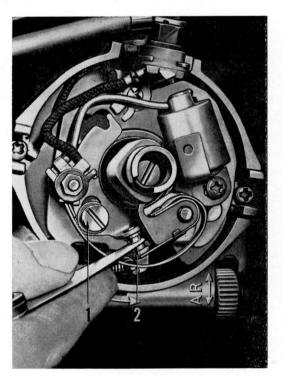

34. CONTACT-BREAKER-POINT GAP ADJUSTMENT

1. Fixed contact-plate locking screw. 2. Check gap with feeler gauge.

The contact-breaker-point gap should be 0·014–0·016 in. when the points are fully open.

The gap setting should be checked and adjusted, if necessary, every 5,000 miles to compensate for wear on the fibre heel of the moving contact lever.

To check the gap setting, remove the distributor cap, lift off the rotor and rotate engine crankshaft until the fibre heel on the moving-contact lever is on the high point of one of the cam lobes. Check gap with feeler gauge.

Where adjustment is required, slacken the fixed-contact locking screw (1) and move the fixed contact until the correct gap setting is obtained. The fixed-contact point can be moved by inserting a screwdriver in the recess provided at the end of the fixed-contact plate and twisting slightly.

When the correct gap has been obtained, securely tighten the locking screw and recheck the gap, as it may have altered slightly when tightening up the screw.

appear to be in good condition, release the moving point, so that the fibre heel is in contact with the high point of the cam lobe and check the contact-breaker point gap. If the gap is incorrect, slacken the fixed contact-point locking screw and by means of a screwdriver located in the notch at the end of the fixed contact point, adjust the gap by moving the point as necessary. Set the gap on the higher limit quoted above, to allow for decrease due to wear on the fibre heel of the moving contact. Once the point gap

35. AUTOLITE TOOL FOR CHECKING AND SETTING SPARKING-PLUG GAP

is correct, tighten the locking screw and recheck the point setting. Before refitting the distributor cap, wipe the inside with a piece of clean, dry rag to remove any oil or condensation which may be present. Similarly, wipe the outside to remove any dirt, as both these may allow tracking to take place, so causing misfiring.

Refacing Contact-breaker Points

To remove the contact-breaker points, unscrew the nut from the terminal post, lift off the two leads and nylon bush. The moving point can now be lifted off its pivot pin. Remove the two fibre washers, one from the pivot pin, the other from the terminal post, unscrew the point-clamping screw and lift off the fixed point.

Where a crater is found on one point and a pip on the other, the points require refacing. The points can be cleaned by facing on a fine oil stone. Take care to keep the points flat when refacing them, so that the faces will meet squarely when the points are closed. The pip can be removed completely but it is not necessary to face off the other point to entirely

remove the crater, as this may remove excess material from the face of the points. After the points have been refaced, they should be wiped clean with a rag moistened with carbon tetra-chloride.

Refit the fixed point, and lightly tighten its securing screw. Fit the fibre washers to the pivot post and terminal post, apply a few drops of oil to the pivot post and refit the moving point. Locate the two leads on the nylon bush, fit the nylon bush to the terminal post and fit and tighten the nut. Adjust the contact-breaker point gap as described previously.

Spark Plugs

The recommended spark plugs are Motorcraft (previously sold under the name of Autolite) 14mm. AG2 on GT models, AG3 on other models. The only satisfactory way of cleaning these plugs is in a sand-blasting machine, so that all carbon can be cleaned from the inside of the plug body. After cleaning the plugs, a fine file should be drawn across the plug points to remove any deposits which may still be present. The plug-point gap should be 0·023 to 0·028 in. To adjust the point gap, only the earth electrode, that is the electrode secured to the plug body, should be adjusted; bend this as necessary to obtain the correct gap. Never attempt to bend the centre electrode as this will fracture the insulation on the plug.

Clean all dirt off the outside of the plugs, fit new washers to them and refit the plugs, tightening them securely. Reconnect the spark-plug leads, connecting them in the correct firing order, which is 1, 2, 4, 3, and check that the leads are tightened securely in the distributor cap.

It may be advantageous to renew the spark plugs every 10,000 miles to maintain the engine at its peak performance.

The spark-plug leads have a carbon-impregnated cotton core to prevent radio and TV interference and no other form of suppressor is required in the ignition circuit.

IGNITION TIMING

The ignition timing is the point at which the high-tension spark occurs, that is, the instant the contact-breaker points open to fire the mixture in the cylinders. This timing, although checked with the engine stationary, is varied to meet both load and speed conditions. As the engine speed increases, it is necessary to fire the mixture earlier, so that maximum cylinder pressures are built up with the piston at top dead centre. At lower engine speeds, the mixture can be fired later, due to the reduced piston speed. This is varied by the centrifugal weights, according to engine speed and by the vacuum unit according to engine load. If the timing is advanced, that is, the spark occurs too early, excessive pressures will be built up in the cylinder, giving pinking and rough running. If the ignition is retarded, i.e. too late, overheating and loss of power will result. The firing order of the engine is 1, 2, 4, 3, No. 1 being the cylinder nearest the radiator.

Checking Ignition-Timing

To check the ignition timing, the position of one of the pistons in its cylinder on compression stroke must first be set. A mark on the rim of the crankshaft pulley and pointers on the left-hand side of the engine-timing cover are used to give this position for either No. 1 or No. 4 piston. At the same time, the contact-breaker points should be checked to see that they are just opening. This is best carried out by inserting a side-lamp bulb in the low-tension circuit, so that when the points open the bulb goes out.

On Standard and De Luxe models, the ignition timing is 8° before top dead centre (B.T.D.C.) and the notch on the crankshaft pulley should be midway between the pointers on the front timing cover to give this setting. The ignition timing on G.T. models is 10° before top dead centre and the notch on the crankshaft pulley should be in line with the upper pointer on the timing cover for this setting.

To set the timing, disconnect No. 1 plug lead and unscrew the spark plug. Rotate the engine, holding one thumb over the plug hole, so that as the piston comes up on compression stroke, air pressure will be felt in the cylinder. Slowly rotate the engine until the notch on the rim of the crankshaft pulley is in correct location to the pointers on the front of the timing cover. Connect the bulb between the SW terminal of the ignition coil and the contact-breaker terminal on the distributor. Adjust the knurled nut on the vacuum-control spindle, so that the fourth line on the graduated scale is just visible. Slacken the clamp screws securing the distributor to the cylinder block and, if the bulb is not illuminated, rotate the body of the distributor *slightly* anti-clockwise until the bulb lights. Then turn the body in the opposite direction until the light just goes out. If the lamp is illuminated, *slightly* turn the distributor body in a clockwise direction until the light just goes out. Take care not to move the body from this setting and retighten the clamp screws.

Where a neon timing light is available, the ignition timing can be checked with the engine idling. Connect the timing light to No. 1 spark plug, or to the contact-breaker terminal, depending on the type of light in use. Shine the light on to the pointers on the front timing cover and adjust the ignition timing by rotating the distributor body until the notch in the crankshaft pulley appears in the correct position to the pointers on the front timing cover. This latter method gives a more accurate setting of the ignition timing as it is done under running conditions.

Identification of Distributors

Due to the different characteristics between the high- and low-compression engines, distributors giving different ignition-advance characteristics are used and should never be interchanged. These can be identified by a coloured washer or marking on the contact-breaker terminal: the high-compression distributor is identified by a brown washer or marking and the low-compression distributor by a yellow washer or marking.

Varying the Timing

Some variation in ignition timing may be called for, depending on the type of fuel in use – this is best checked on the road. A low-compression engine operating on regular fuel would 'pink' under load if the ignition was too far advanced. To check this accelerate hard from 30 to 50 m.p.h. with the throttle wide open. If the engine does not pink, advance the ignition by rotating the knurled nut on the vacuum-

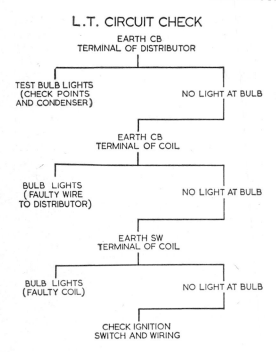

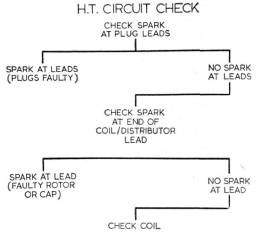

control spindle in the direction of the arrow marked 'A' until the engine pinks on test; then turn the nut in the direction of the arrow marked 'R' until the pinking is just eliminated. This will give the best ignition setting.

With a high-compression engine operating on premium-grade fuel, this cannot be done as 'pinking' does not occur. The ignition timing, however, can be too far advanced and will reduce engine performance. To check this setting, again accelerate in a top gear from 30 to 50 m.p.h. and check the time taken for this. Adjust the ignition timing until the time taken on this test is reduced to a minimum. This again will give the optimum ignition setting. When carrying out either of these tests, they must of course be done under exactly the same conditions to obtain the correct ignition timing.

IGNITION-SYSTEM FAULT LOCATION

Any fault in the ignition system will produce one of the following defects:

(*a*) Difficult starting   (*c*) Erratic running
(*b*) Loss of power   (*d*) Overheating.

D

To check the ignition system for faults (*a*), (*b*) and (*c*), disconnect one spark-plug lead, switch on the ignition, hold the lead approximately ¼ in. from the cylinder block and turn the engine with the starter motor. This can be done, except on cars fitted with automatic transmission, by depressing the rubber button on the end of the starter-motor switch in the engine compartment, first making sure the car is out of gear. The spark should jump the gap from the end of the plug lead to the cylinder block and should be a bluish colour. If the spark appears weak or no spark is visible, check the low-tension circuit.

With ignition on and contact breaker open, connect a bulb between contact-breaker plate terminal and cylinder block; if bulb lights, the low-tension circuit is complete to this point. Where the bulb does not light, connect it between the CB terminal of the coil and earth. If the bulb lights, it indicates a broken wire between the CB terminal of the coil and the contact-breaker plate terminal. Where the bulb does not light, connect it between the SW terminal of the coil and earth. If the bulb now lights it indicates a fault in the low-tension winding of the coil; if the bulb does not light it indicates a fault in the ignition switch or wiring.

This can be checked simply by connecting a lead from the negative terminal of the battery to the SW terminal of the ignition coil, so by-passing the switch and its associated wiring.

Where the bulb lights when connected between the contact-breaker plate terminal and earth, it indicates that the low-tension circuit is complete to this point and the contact-breaker points should be removed and checked. If the points are found to be badly burnt and pitted, this is an indication of a faulty condenser and the points should be refaced, or renewed if badly burnt, and a new condenser fitted. After refacing or renewing the points, readjust the contact-breaker point gap.

Where a spark was visible at the end of the plug lead when carrying out the initial test, remove and clean all spark plugs.

If the low-tension circuit is complete, but no spark is obtained at the plug lead, disconnect the lead between the coil and distributor cap (at the cap) by unscrewing the plastic nut under the rubber sleeve in the centre of the cap. Do not lose the small copper washer from the end of the lead as this retains the lead in position when the nut is tightened. Hold the end of this lead $\frac{1}{4}$ in. from the cylinder block and again crank the engine on the starter motor. If there is a spark at the end of this lead, but nothing at the end of the plug lead, it indicates either a faulty rotor or a cracked distributor cap. Inspection of these two components will indicate any cracking. If there is no spark at the end of this high-tension lead, and the low-tension circuit is correct, it indicates a fault in the ignition coil which must be replaced.

The ignition timing can be checked after these operations are complete, but this is not going to vary, certainly not sufficiently to cause bad or difficult starting. Variation in ignition timing will be noticeable in engine performance.

Overheating

This is invariably an indication of retarded ignition and the ignition timing must be checked and adjusted as described previously.

Chapter 8

CLUTCH

AN hydraulically operated single dry-plate 7¼-in. diameter clutch is fitted to the Consul Corsair. The friction facings are flexibly mounted to each side of the centre plate, which has a spring-loaded hub to assist in a smooth take up of the drive. A pre-lubricated bush, fitted in the flywheel, supports the spigot of the main-drive gear which is splined into the hub of the clutch disc. The clutch pressure plate is located on the face of the flywheel by three dowels and secured with six bolts and lock washers.

A combined fluid reservoir and master cylinder is mounted on the engine side of the bulkhead and operated by a pendant pedal. The master cylinder is connected by a flexible pipe to the slave cylinder, secured to the flywheel housing. The slave cylinder operates the clutch-release bearing through a push-rod and relay arm pivoted on a fulcrum pin in the front face of the gearbox.

When the clutch pedal is depressed, fluid is forced from the master cylinder to the slave cylinder, and pressure on the slave-cylinder piston operates the release arm through the push-rod. The inner end of the release arm is located behind the clutch-release bearing and

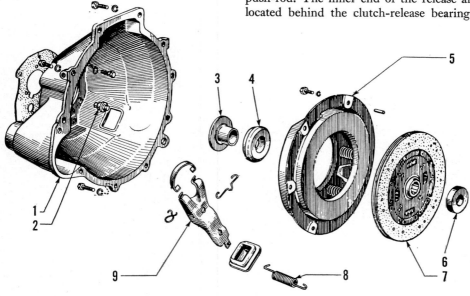

36. EXPLODED VIEW OF CLUTCH

1. Clutch bellhousing
2. Release-arm pivot
3. Release-bearing sleeve
4. Release bearing
5. Clutch cover and pressure plate assembly
6. Pilot bush in flywheel
7. Driven plate
8. Release-arm retracting spring
9. Clutch release arm

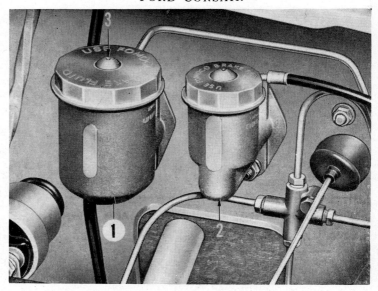

37. CLUTCH- AND BRAKE-FLUID RESERVOIRS

1. Brake master cylinder. **2.** Clutch master cylinder. **3.** Vent hole.

The clutch- and brake-fluid reservoirs are integral with their master cylinders located in the engine compartment on the driver's side of the car.

Every 5,000 miles, the level of the fluid in both reservoirs should be checked to ensure that it is up to the marking on the outside of the casing. This is approximately $\frac{5}{8}$ in. below the top of each reservoir.

When topping up the reservoirs, use only the correct type of fluid serviced under Part No. ME3833E. Before removing the caps, wipe them and the reservoirs with clean rag to prevent any possibility of dirt entering the systems. Do not use rag that is contaminated with petrol, paraffin or grease. Use only a clean container when topping up.

Before refitting the reservoir caps, check that the bleed hole in each cap is clear.

as the arm is operated, the release bearing is pushed forward into contact with the clutch fingers on the pressure plate, so relieving the pressure and disengaging the clutch disc.

MAINTENANCE OF CLUTCH ASSEMBLY

The only maintenance called for on the clutch assembly is to check the level of fluid in the master cylinder and the release-arm free movement after the first 500 miles and, subsequently, at every 5,000 miles.

Clutch-fluid Reservoir

To check the clutch-fluid reservoir, remove the cap from the reservoir and check that the level of fluid is up to the marking on the outside of the casing. This is approximately $\frac{5}{8}$ in. below the top of the reservoir. Before removing the cap, wipe both the cap and the outside of the reservoir, taking care not to push any dirt into the bleed hole in the cap. Use only clean rag for this, as any mineral oil contamination of the fluid will damage the seals in the master and slave cylinders. If it is necessary to add fluid to the reservoir, only the correct type serviced under Part No. ME3833E should be used. At the same time only a clean container should be used for this fluid to prevent contamination and damage to the seals. Before refitting the reservoir cap, check that the bleed hole is clear and unobstructed.

Clutch-release-arm Free Movement

The clutch-release arm free movement should also be checked at the first 500 miles, then at every 5,000-mile service; this should be $\frac{1}{10}$ in. and is measured between the release arm and the domed nut on the operating-cylinder push-rod.

To check this adjustment, disconnect the retracting spring fitted to the end of the release arm and push and pull on the end of the arm. If the clearance is incorrect, hold the push-rod,

clutch release-arm free movement, that is, too much free movement. Check and adjust this if necessary. If the release-arm free movement is correct and spin is still experienced, check that, whilst someone depresses the clutch pedal, the release arm is moving fully forward.

If the release-arm movement is not satis-

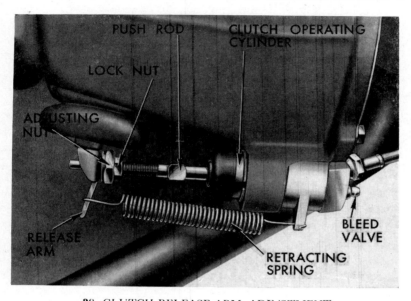

38. CLUTCH-RELEASE-ARM ADJUSTMENT

The clutch-release arm, operated by the hydraulic slave (operating) cylinder via the push rod, should have a free movement of $\frac{1}{10}$ in.

To check this clearance, disconnect retracting spring from the release arm and push and pull on the end of the arm. If adjustment is required, hold the push rod, slacken the locknut and turn the adjusting nut until the correct clearance is obtained. Retighten locknut and reconnect retracting spring.

slacken the locknut and adjust the domed nut as necessary to give the correct clearance. Once this has been established, retighten the locknut to prevent this setting altering in service and refit the spring. At the same time as the release-arm free movement is adjusted (whilst still under the vehicle), check the pipe for leaks and also inspect the slave cylinder for signs of leaks.

CLUTCH FAULTS

Clutch faults are (*a*) spin, (*b*) slip and (*c*) judder.

Clutch Spin

If the clutch is spinning, difficulty will be experienced in engaging gear, particularly from a standstill. This may be due to an incorrect

factory, it indicates a fault in either the clutch master cylinder or slave cylinder – either of these may be leaking. To check for this on the master cylinder, release the rubber boot around the operating push-rod and if the master-cylinder seal is leaking, operating fluid will be found in the rubber boot. The clutch slave cylinder can be checked for leaks in a similar manner. If these three points are correct and spin is still experienced, the clutch unit must be dismantled to check the condition of the pressure plate and also that the disc is free to move on the main-drive gear splines.

Clutch Slip

Clutch slip, as its name indicates, occurs when

insufficient pressure is being applied by the clutch pressure plate. To check for this condition, drive the car and, holding the accelerator pedal steady, apply the footbrake. The engine speed should decrease as the car slows down; if there is little change in engine speed, it indicates that the clutch is slipping.

The main cause of clutch slip is generally insufficient release-arm free travel and this should be checked and adjusted if necessary. Provided the release-arm free travel is correct, slip may be due to oil or grease on the clutch disc or a faulty clutch pressure plate and, again, the clutch will have to be dismantled to rectify the trouble. Slight clutch slip can occur if the driver's foot is rested on the pedal when driving and even if the pressure is insufficient to cause clutch slip, the release bearing will be held in contact with the pressure-plate fingers, giving short life of the clutch-release bearing.

Clutch Judder

Clutch judder is the term used to describe the shuddering which may be experienced, particularly in reverse gear or in starting from rest in first gear. It is generally due to loose or worn engine mountings, oil or grease on the clutch disc or an incorrectly adjusted clutch pressure plate.

Where the engine mountings are found to be tight and in good condition, the clutch will have to be removed from the engine and examined.

Worn Release Bearing

A worn release bearing is generally indicated by a noise when the pedal is lightly depressed, just sufficient to hold the bearing in contact with the pressure-plate fingers. The gearbox must be removed from the vehicle to fit a new release bearing.

Whenever the gearbox or engine are removed from the car, the clutch disc and release bearing should be checked and renewed, if necessary, to avoid further dismantling at a later date to renew only these components.

Chapter 9

GEARBOX, PROPELLER SHAFT AND REAR AXLE

POWER is transmitted through a four-speed fully-synchronized gearbox (for optional automatic transmission, see later) to an open-drive propeller shaft connected to a hypoid semi-floating rear axle. The synchronizers are of the blocker-type which prevent gear engagement until the gear speeds are fully synchronized. An extended mainshaft is fitted, this being supported on (1) needle-roller bearings in the main-drive gear into which the shaft is spigoted, (2) by a ball-bearing in the front of the extension housing, and (3) at the rear by the yoke of the universal joint which, in turn, is supported by a white-metal bush fitted in the extension housing. An oil breather is incorporated in one of the gear-lever housing retaining bolts.

Two types of gearshift mechanism are used on these cars: floor-mounted remote control on G.T. and optionally fitted to De Luxe models

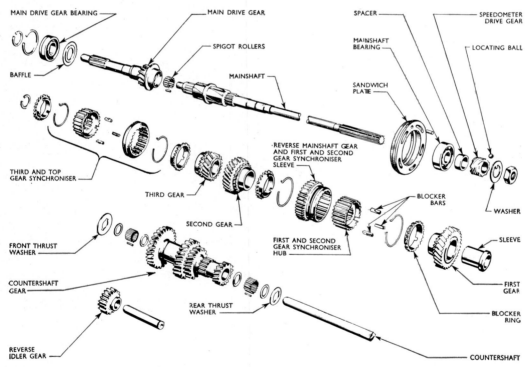

39. SHAFTS AND GEARS IN SYNCHROMESH GEARBOX
The first-gear sleeve is locked to the mainshaft by a locating ball.

or a remote control which operates through cables mounted on the steering column on Standard and De Luxe models.

The gear-lever positions are inscribed on the floor-mounted control: moving the lever to the left and forward engages first gear, to the left and back engages second gear, third and fourth gears are in the corresponding positions and are engaged after moving the lever to the right. Reverse gear is engaged by lifting the lever,

engagement of reverse gear. To overcome this, sharply tap the gear lever away from the steering wheel, reverse can then be engaged by moving it anti-clockwise.

No lubrication or maintenance is required on either of these types of gear-shift mechanisms.

The open-drive propeller shaft is fitted with two universal joints, and is of constant length. Movement of the shaft due to rear-axle deflection is accommodated by the front yoke of the

40. GEAR-LEVER POSITIONS – STEERING-COLUMN CHANGE

41. GEAR-LEVER POSITIONS – FLOOR CHANGE

moving it as far left as possible, then back as for second and fourth gear.

On the early models, the remote-control lever is biased towards the first- and second-gear positions when in neutral and a slight pressure should be kept on the lever to hold it towards the right when changing between third and fourth gears.

In January 1964 this was changed so that the lever is now biased towards the third and top positions and the lever should be held lightly towards the left when changing between first and second gears.

The remote-control steering-column change lever is spring-loaded towards the third and top gear positions. To engage first gear, pull the lever up towards the steering wheel and move it clockwise, second gear is engaged by holding the lever towards the wheel and moving it anti-clockwise. Third and fourth gears are in the corresponding positions to first and second gears respectively with the lever in its normal position away from the steering wheel. A spring-loaded stop prevents the accidental

drive shaft sliding on the splines of the gearbox mainshaft.

A pressed-steel banjo-type rear-axle casing is fitted, the hypoid crownwheel and pinion being mounted in the differential carrier, which in turn is bolted to the front face of the axle casing. The rear-axle ratio, which is the ratio between the number of crownwheel teeth and bevel-pinion teeth is 3·9:1 with an optional ratio of 4·125:1 for Standard and De Luxe models. The axle shafts are flanged at their outer ends, the brake drums being bolted to these flanges. The inner ends of the axle shafts are splined into the axle-shaft gears. Pre-lubricated hub bearings are pressed on to the axle shafts and retained by a steel ring at the outer end of the shafts, the bearings being secured by a retainer bolted to the axle casing.

GEARBOX MAINTENANCE

At the first 500 miles, at 10,000 miles and each subsequent 5,000-mile service, the gearbox oil level should be checked. The oil should be changed at the first 5,000-mile service, this

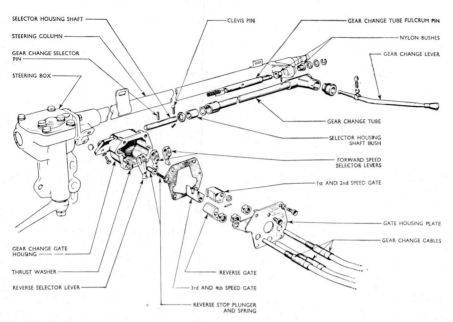

42. ARRANGEMENT OF GEAR-CHANGE CONTROLS – STEERING-COLUMN CHANGE

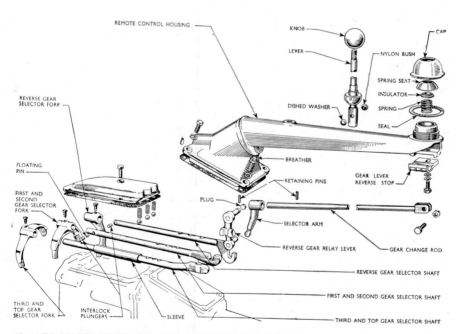

43. ARRANGEMENT OF GEAR-CHANGE CONTROLS – FLOOR CHANGE

GEARBOX RATIOS

First	..	..	..	..	3·543:1
Second	..	..	..	..	2·396:1
Third	..	..	..	..	1·412:1
Fourth	..	..	..	..	1·000:1
Reverse	..	..	..	..	3·963:1

being the only time it is necessary to drain the gearbox. An extreme-pressure lubricant of SAE.80 should be used in the gearbox, which has a capacity of $1\frac{3}{4}$ pints.

A combined filler and level plug is located on the near side of the gearbox and the oil level should be checked at this point. Unscrew the plug and check the oil level, which should be to the level of the plug. If the oil level is low, add oil through the plug hole to bring the level of the oil just to the level of the plug. Do not overfill the gearbox, as this oil may then leak into the clutch housing and damage the linings. After adding oil, allow the surplus to drain off

44. GEARBOX DRAIN AND FILLER PLUGS – MANUAL GEARBOX

before refitting the combined filler and level plug.

After the first 5,000 miles the gearbox should be drained and the box refilled with new oil. This operation is best carried out when the oil is warm to allow complete draining. Place a suitable container under the gearbox and unscrew the drain plug. Allow all the oil to drain out and then refit the drain plug, tighten-

ing it securely. Remove the combined level and filler plug and fill the gearbox to this level. Allow the surplus oil to drain off before refitting the filler and oil-level plug, tightening it securely. At each subsequent 5,000-mile service it is only necessary to check the oil level.

AUTOMATIC TRANSMISSION

The automatic transmission optionally fitted to the Consul Corsair is the Borg-Warner type 35 in which a torque converter transmits engine power to a fully-automatic three-speed and reverse gearbox.

Both upward and downward gear changes are made automatically, the point at which these occur depends on the accelerator pedal position and the road speed. If the throttle pedal is fully depressed to give maximum acceleration, the upward gear changes will be made at a higher road speed than when the pedal is only lightly depressed. The box incorporates an overriding control so that the driver can hold first or second gear up to any road speed if he so wishes, or can change to a lower gear if necessary regardless of road speed.

A selector lever mounted on the steering column controls the automatic transmission and a quadrant below the steering wheel indicates the driving range selected being marked L.D.N.R.P.

Driving Ranges

L – Lock up. – When the selector lever is in this position, the automatic gear changing is overriden, so that when starting from rest in this position, first gear is held permanently engaged and the change to second gear will not be made until the lever is moved to select D. Maximum engine braking is available when the gearbox is locked in first gear. If when driving in top gear in the D range L is selected, the gearbox will change down to second gear and this gear will then be locked in and the change to top can only be made by again selecting D.

Moderate engine braking is available when second gear is locked in and as the road speed drops to approximately 5 m.p.h., the gearbox will automatically change down to first gear which is then locked in as described previously.

Use of the L range overrides the automatic gear changing so that the gearbox is virtually used as a normal manual-change box although, of course, there is no clutch action to carry out.

D – Drive. – This is the normal driving range and, when selected, fully automatic gear changes are made. When starting from rest in this range, the car will start off in first gear and automatically change up to second and top gears as the road speed increases. The speeds at which these changes will be made depends on the accelerator pedal position – so that if a driver wants maximum acceleration, the upward changes will be made at a higher road speed than when the car is driven more gently. As the road speed drops, when hill climbing, the downward changes to second and first gears will be made automatically.

These downward changes can also be induced by the driver depressing the throttle pedal to the limit of its travel 'the kick-down position'.

If when travelling in top gear and maximum acceleration is required for overtaking, the change to second can be made by pressing the pedal to the kick-down position. The change to second gear will be made automatically provided the road speed is not above the maximum in second gear, approximately 58 m.p.h., and an automatic change to top gear will again be made at this speed.

The change from second to first gear can be made in a similar manner, provided the road speed in second gear is not more than approximately 38 m.p.h.

N – Neutral. – This is as the normal neutral position on any gearbox, the automatic transmission being disconnected in this range. The engine can only be started in N or P and either of these should be selected if the engine is to be allowed to idle for a long period, as when carrying out any adjustments.

R – Reverse. This is the reverse-gear position, engine braking being available in this gear. Only select R with the car stationary.

P – Park. – When the selector lever is in this position, the gearbox is in neutral as in N but, at the same time, the transmission is locked mechanically. The engine can be started when the lever is in this position and can be idled for long periods. It is advisable to only select P

when the car is stationary or damage may occur as the mechanical lock is engaged.

Driving the Car

The starter is operated by turning the ignition key fully clockwise but on these cars an additional isolating switch is incorporated in the circuit and is controlled by the selector lever. Place the selector lever in the N or P position to close the isolating switch and turn the ignition key fully clockwise to start the engine. If it is found at any time that the engine can be started with the lever in any other position than N or P, the isolating switch should be adjusted by your dealer. This switch has two additional terminals through which a reversing lamp can be wired and which will be automatically switched on when R is selected.

When starting the engine with the choke, the idling speed will be higher than normal, and the car will move when one of the driving ranges is selected. To prevent this apply the footbrake firmly before moving the selector lever, release the handbrake and the car can be controlled on the footbrake without touching the throttle pedal.

If, at any time, the engine will not start, the car should not be towed in an attempt to do this, but pushed by another vehicle. To do this, select N and when the speed reaches approximately 25 m.p.h. switch on the ignition and move the selector lever to D. It will be seen that if the car is towed to get an emergency start it may collide with the towing vehicle under these circumstances. Any time it is necessary to tow the car other than to start the engine, this can be done with the selector lever in N provided that the breakdown is not in the automatic transmission. If the transmission is faulty, the drive shaft must be disconnected before towing or further damage may result.

An additional advantage of this type of transmission is that if at any time the car gets stuck in soft ground or snow it can be rocked backward and forward to extricate it. This can be done by lightly depressing the throttle pedal to give a fast idling speed then alternately selecting R and D whilst maintaining a constant engine speed. The changes must be made as quickly as possible – select R as the car is

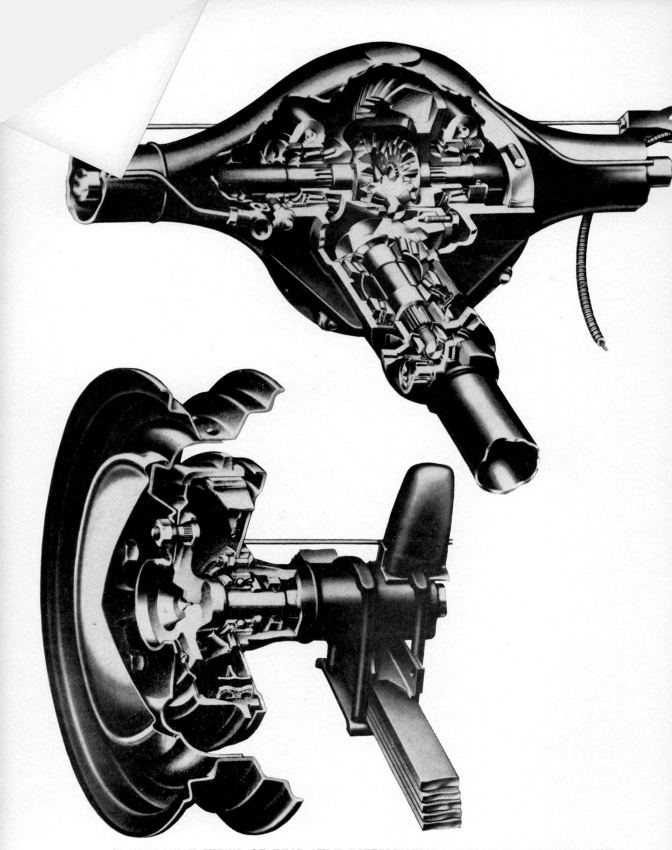

45. CUT-AWAY VIEWS OF REAR-AXLE DIFFERENTIAL ASSEMBLY AND REAR HUB

moving forward, trying to do this just before wheel spin starts and select D at the same point as the car is moving backwards. In this way the car can be rocked to extricate itself.

This is the only time that R should be engaged with the car moving forwards, normally the car should be stopped before selecting R.

Routine Maintenance

Apart from checking the fluid level every 5,000 miles, no maintenance is required on the automatic transmission. The fluid level should be checked with the car standing on level ground and the transmission at its normal working temperature which is established after driving approximately five miles.

To check the fluid level, select P and allow the engine to idle for two minutes, then with the engine still idling in P withdraw the dipstick from the filler tube at the right-hand rear of the engine compartment. Wipe the dipstick with a piece of non-fluffy rag or paper tissue, insert the dipstick in the tube, push it right home and withdraw it immediately. Add fluid if necessary to bring the level to the 'Full' mark on the dipstick. The amount necessary can be judged as 1 pint is required to raise the level from the 'Low' to the 'Full' mark. Do not overfill the transmission.

If for any reason the transmission fluid level is checked when the transmission is cold, the level should be approximately $\frac{3}{8}$ in. below the 'Full' mark to allow for expansion as the transmission fluid warms up.

Automatic-transmission fluid must be kept clean and only clean containers used when adding fluid. The dipstick should never be wiped with fluffy rag or particles may be transferred to the transmission, possibly causing trouble later.

It is essential that only the correct fluid is used in the transmission – this must be an Armour qualified Type A, Suffix A, Automatic Transmission Fluid.

There is no need to drain the fluid from the automatic transmission during normal servicing. The fluid is cooled by air passing over the gearbox oil pan and occasionally the oil pan should be cleaned to remove any mud and dirt which may have collected, as this may cause overheating of the fluid.

PROPELLER-SHAFT MAINTENANCE

The drive-shaft universal joints are pre-packed with lubricant and sealed so that no lubrication is called for throughout their life.

Occasionally check the security of the self-locking nuts retaining the rear universal-joint flange to the rear-axle pinion flange. Normally these nuts require little attention but if, however, they are found to have worked loose, new self-locking nuts should be fitted.

The front yoke of the front universal joint is splined to the gearbox mainshaft. An oil seal is fitted in the rear of the gearbox extension housing to prevent leakage at this point. If oil leakage is found around the end of the extension housing, the oil seal should be renewed.

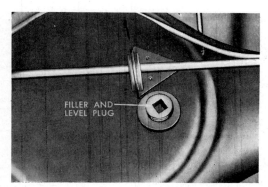

46. REAR-AXLE FILLER AND LEVEL PLUG

REAR-HUB BEARINGS

The rear hub bearings are pre-lubricated and sealed, and do not require lubrication throughout their life. A check on their condition can be made by attempting to rock and lift the rear wheel when the car is jacked up. Any movement at this point may be an indication that the hub bearings are worn.

REAR-AXLE MAINTENANCE

A combined filler and level plug is fitted in the rear-axle casing. At the first 500-mile and every following 5,000-mile service, this plug should be removed and the oil level checked. The oil level should just be to the level of the plug. If necessary, add oil to bring it to this level, allowing the surplus to drain off before refitting the combined filler and level plug. It is essential that only a SAE.90 hypoid lubricant is used in the rear axle. An ordinary gear oil, if used in the rear axle, would result in rapid wear and damage to the gears. It is not necessary to drain the oil from the axle throughout its life, so no drain plug is fitted.

TRANSMISSION FAULTS

Little trouble will be experienced with the transmission system, provided that the lubrication is carried out correctly as described above. If difficulty is experienced in changing gear, check the clutch release-arm free travel as described in the previous chapter. If free travel is excessive, the clutch will not release fully, consequently causing difficult gear changing. This will be most noticeably when engaging first or reverse gear with the vehicle stationary.

If, however, the gear engagement is satisfactory when the car is stationary, but noisy or difficult engagement is made when changing gear with the car in motion, this is generally an indication of worn synchronizer cones. The gearbox must be dismantled to renew synchronizer cones.

After a high mileage has been covered and wear has occurred between the mating parts, the gearbox will tend to become more noisy; this increased noise coupled with possible difficult gear changing is a definite indication that the gearbox should be overhauled.

Similarly, wear between the crownwheel and pinion in the rear axle will occur, giving an increased clearance between these gears. This increased backlash may be noticeable as a clonk when taking up the drive from stationary or by a whine when the car is on the over-run. The axle is fully adjustable for this condition, but these adjustments are very critical and should never be attempted unless the special equipment developed for this purpose is available.

Chapter 10

STEERING

A RECIRCULATORY-BALL worm-and-nut steering box, having a ratio in the straight-ahead position of 15·1:1 on Standard and De Luxe cars and 13·4:1 on G.T. models, is fitted to these vehicles. The rocker shaft is located in bushes in the box, its upper end being connected to the nut whilst the lower end is secured to the drop arm. Movement of the steering wheel and shaft screws the nut up or down the shaft so pivoting the rocker shaft in its bushes and rotating the drop arm. The steering box is secured to the right-hand frame member, an idler arm being fitted in the corresponding position on the left-hand frame member.

A connecting rod is fitted between the drop arm and idler arm, individual track rods are fitted between this and the steering arms which are bolted to the foot of each front-suspension unit. The wheel spindle is forged integral with the suspension-unit foot. Movement of the steering wheel and drop arm is transferred through this linkage to each road wheel. Ball joints are fitted at each end of the track rods and rubber-bushed studs at each end of the drop-arm to idler-arm rod.

The suspension units consist of a vertical double-acting shock absorber, the upper end of

the piston rod being located on a double-row ball thrust bearing mounted in rubber to the upper-support member. The upper-support members are in turn bolted to a reinforcement bracket inside each front-wheel arch. Large-diameter coil springs surround each piston rod, the lower end of each spring resting on a spring seat welded to the suspension unit, the upper end being retained by a seat fitted on the piston rod and held in position by the top mounting. Track-control arms, the inner ends of which are located in rubber bushes in the front cross-member, are connected by ball joints to the foot of each suspension unit and retain the steering alignment laterally.

A stabilizer bar retains the steering alignment longitudinally; the ends of the bar being mounted in rubber bushes in each track-control arm, the bar being secured at the front in rubber bushes to the body sidemembers.

Steering lock stops, which contact abutments on the drop-arm to idler-arm rod, are fitted on the engine-support crossmember. Apart from toe-in and toe-out on turns, all steering angles are pre-determined in manufacture and are non-adjustable.

CHECKING BOLT TIGHTNESS

Every 5,000 miles, check the tightness of the bolts securing the front crossmember to the frame sidemembers.

RENEWING BALL-JOINT PLASTIC GAITERS

All steering-linkage ball joints work in plastic seatings which do not require lubrication after assembly. The ball joints are pre-lubricated and sealed by a plastic gaiter. Every 5,000 miles inspect the gaiters for damage; if split or torn, they must be renewed.

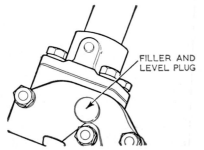

FILLER AND LEVEL PLUG

47. STEERING-BOX OIL-FILLER AND OIL-LEVEL RUBBER PLUG

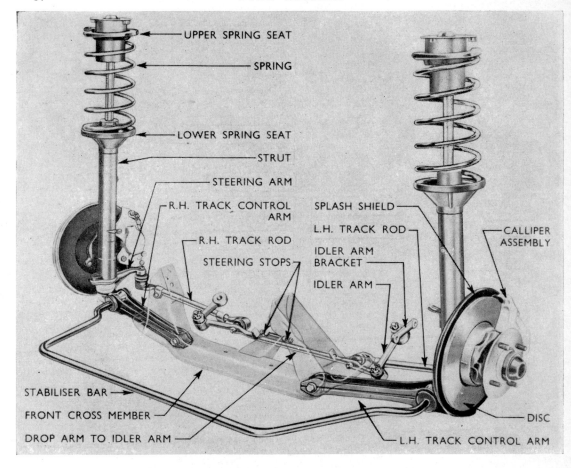

UPPER SPRING SEAT

SPRING

LOWER SPRING SEAT

STRUT

STEERING ARM

R.H. TRACK CONTROL ARM

R.H. TRACK ROD

STEERING STOPS

SPLASH SHIELD

L.H. TRACK ROD

IDLER ARM BRACKET

IDLER ARM

CALLIPER ASSEMBLY

STABILISER BAR

FRONT CROSS MEMBER

DROP ARM TO IDLER ARM

DISC

L.H. TRACK CONTROL ARM

48. LAYOUT OF STEERING LINKAGE AND FRONT SUSPENSION

To renew these gaiters, disconnect the ball joint, remove the gaiter retainer and pull off the gaiter. After renewing the gaiter, secure it in place with the retainer, taking care that this is fitted correctly, and reconnect the ball joint. Tighten the castellated nut securely and lock it with a new split pin. As each ball-joint gaiter is examined, the condition of the joint can be checked by pushing and pulling on the rod in line with the ball joint. Slight movement may be felt, but if this is excessive the joint should be renewed. At the same time, this wear on the ball joints will be noticeable by the increased free play on the steering wheel.

ATTENTION TO STEERING BOX

The steering box oil level should be checked at the first 500 miles and every 5,000 miles. To do this, remove the rubber plug fitted to the steering-box cover and the oil should be to this level. If necessary, add SAE.90 E.P. gear oil to bring it to this level. Replace the rubber plug securely.

Apart from the normal 5,000-mile lubrication service, the steering box requires no regular maintenance. Occasionally, a check on the steering-shaft adjustment can be made by lifting at the steering wheel and a check on the rocker shaft and float adjustment by pulling and pushing at the end of the rocker shaft. If there is excessive movment at these points, it is an indication that general wear has taken place throughout the steering box. Adjustments to the steering box should be carried out by the garage.

FRONT HUBS

The front hubs are mounted on taper-roller bearings and their adjustment should be checked every 5,000 miles. At every 15,000 miles, the hubs should be removed and the bearings cleaned and repacked with fresh lithium-based grease.

Adjusting Wheel-hub Bearings

To check the bearing adjustment, jack up the car and check the end-float on the bearings by pushing and pulling on the horizontal centre line of the wheel. If the end-float is excessive, the bearings should be adjusted. To do this, remove the road wheel and brake pads as described in Chapter 12, lever dust cap out of hub, withdraw split pin and remove castellated retainer from the adjusting nut. Rotate the hub and disc assembly, at the same time tightening the adjusting nut until a heavy drag can be felt on the disc. Fit the castellated retainer to the adjusting nut so that one slot lines up with the split-pin hole in the wheel spindle. Slacken the adjusting nut one castellation at a time until the hub and disc turn freely and a slight end-float can just be felt on the hub. Fit a new split pin, opening both legs to lock the adjustment. Refit the dust cap, brake pads in their original location, and road wheels. The dust cap must be fitted dry – not packed with grease.

Replacing Hub Bearings with Grease

Every 15,000 miles, the front-hub bearings should be removed, cleaned and repacked with lithium-based grease. To do this, the brake calipers must be removed; these can be removed with the pads in place. Jack up the car and remove the road wheels. Slacken the locknut retaining the flexible brake pipe to the suspension leg and disengage the pipe from the bracket. It is not necessary to break the hydraulic connection at this point. Straighten the tabs on the two caliper-retaining bolts, unscrew the bolts and remove the caliper. Support the caliper to prevent straining the hydraulic pipes.

Lever the dust cap out of the hub, remove the split pin and adjusting-nut retainer and screw off the adjusting nut. Pull off the bearing thrust washer and remove the outer wheel bearing.

The hub and disc assembly can now be withdrawn from the wheel spindle. The inner hub bearing is retained in position by a grease retainer; this can be levered out of its seating and the bearing lifted out of the bearing cup.

Clean the old grease out of the hub, and repack the hub with fresh grease. If a lithium-based grease is used, the hub should not be packed completely full but appreciable room left for expansion due to heat. If the hub is completely filled with grease, this will be forced out by expansion and may get on to the brake disc or linings causing erratic or poor braking. Wash the old grease out of the inner bearing, that is, the larger bearing. Dry the bearing and repack it with grease, working the grease well into the bearing rollers. Fit the bearing to its cup in the hub and fit a new grease seal with the sharp edge of the seal towards the bearing. Similarly, clean and lubricate the outer bearing.

Fit the hub and disc assembly to the wheel spindle, install the outer bearing and thrust washer and fit the bearing-adjusting nut.

Adjust the hub bearings as described previously. Lever the brake pads apart to push the pistons into the cylinders, as this will allow them to slide over the disc more easily. Locate the caliper on the spindle with its mounting flange behind the spindle flange. Fit a new locking plate to the two retaining bolts, fit and tighten the bolts to 40–45 lb-ft. torque and bend up the locking tabs to lock securely on one flat on each bolt head. Refit the hydraulic pipe to the bracket on the suspension leg and tighten the locknut. If the hydraulic-pipe connections have been broken, the braking system must be bled as described in Chapter 12.

Refit the road wheels, lower the car to the ground, and finally check the tightness of the wheel nuts. Pump the brake pedal a few times until it becomes firm to relocate the brake pads in their operating position.

STEERING TROUBLES

Steering troubles are normally indicated by uneven or heavy front tyre wear. Occasionally inspect the tyres for this uneven wear, and if feathering, that is wear on either the inner or outer edges of the tyre tread, is noticed, the wheel alignment should be checked. Similarly,

E

when checking the steering of the car, ensure that the tyres are evenly worn and correctly mated, and inflated to the correct pressures. At the same time, check the front-wheel bearing adjustment and adjust this if necessary.

Due to the working clearances in the joints on the steering linkage, some free play can be felt at the rim of the steering wheel; this will increase as wear takes place on the steering joints. If it is necessary to check for excessive free play at the steering-wheel rim, the wheel should be moved slowly backwards and forwards between the limits of its free play, whilst at the same time the linkage is inspected to determine the points at which wear has taken place.

TOE-IN OF FRONT WHEELS

If, as described previously, the front tyres are excessively or unevenly worn, the wheel alignment should be checked. All steering angles are set in manufacture, the only adjustment being on the toe-in and toe-out on turns. The toe-in should be $\frac{1}{16}-\frac{1}{8}$ in., that is, with the wheels in the straight-ahead position, the distance between the high points of the tyre walls measured on the centre line of the wheels at the rear should be $\frac{1}{16}-\frac{1}{8}$ in. more than the measurement taken at the corresponding point at the front of the wheels. This adjustment requires careful and accurate measurement and is best left to the expert.

WHEEL BALANCE

Independent front-wheel suspension is sensitive to wheel balance and any out-of-balance condition on the road wheels, which may be due to unevenly worn tyres, can give rise to tremor or shimmy which may be felt on the steering wheel. Where this is experienced, the wheels should be balanced to eliminate the cause of the trouble.

Chapter 11

FRONT AND REAR SUSPENSION

AS described in the previous chapter, the independent front-suspension units consist of a vertical, double-acting, shock absorber with a large coil spring fitted around the piston rod of the shock absorber and located between a seat on the shock-absorber body and its upper-mounting member. Vertical movement of the road wheel forces the shock-absorber body upwards against the resistance of the coil spring and the internal resistance of the shock absorber. Fluid is forced through valves in the shock absorber from the inner to outer cylinder. On the downward stroke, the road spring forces the shock-absorber body down against resistance again offered by fluid being transferred from the internal cylinders, so damping out the spring oscillations.

REAR SUSPENSION

The rear axle is mounted on underslung longitudinal semi-elliptic springs, double-acting telescopic shock absorbers being fitted. On G.T. models from October 1964, rubber-bushed radius arms are fitted between the axle and body sidemembers.

The action of the rear shock absorbers is similar to that of the front – on the compression stroke fluid is forced from one cylinder to the other cylinder, and on the rebound or downward stroke the fluid is transferred from the second cylinder to the first cylinder.

SHOCK ABSORBERS

Both front and rear shock absorbers are sealed units and, provided the seals are not leaking, there should be little necessity to add fluid. (Note that no provision is made for topping up telescopic rear shock absorbers – if faulty they should be replaced.)

On the front shock absorbers, an oil seal is fitted round the piston rod at the top of the shock-absorber body and this seal should be renewed if there is excessive leakage at this point. This area is normally slightly damp with fluid but any quantity of fluid indicates that the seal is leaking.

On the rear shock absorbers a similar oil seal is fitted in the body around the piston rod. Where there is excessive leakage of fluid at this point, a reconditioned shock absorber must be fitted.

Topping up Front Shock Absorbers

Every 15,000 miles or if the front shock absorbers are found to be leaking, the fluid level can be checked at the combined filler and level plug which is fitted in each shock absorber; the plug is located approximately 3 in. below the bottom spring seat. On one side of the vehicle this will be found facing towards the front, but towards the rear on the other side of the car. When checking the shock-absorber fluid level, the car must be standing on level ground in the normal unladen position. Never force fluid into the shock absorbers under pressure. Use only the correct fluid which is serviced under part No. M100502-E. Do not use engine oil in its place.

To check the front shock-absorber fluid level, clean the surface of the shock absorber around the filler plug to prevent road dirt or grit getting into the shock absorber and then unscrew the filler plug. The fluid level should be just to the level of the plug. If necessary, add the correct fluid until it just runs from the filler-plug hole. Allow the surplus fluid to drain away, refit the plug and wipe any surplus fluid off the shock-absorber body.

The seals should be renewed if the leaks are excessive, to prevent internal damage to the unit through an excessively low-fluid level.

Rear Shock-absorber Mountings

The telescopic rear shock absorbers are mounted vertically between the axle and the body, the upper end of each one being secured to a body member which is visible at the front of the luggage boot. A rubber bush is fitted in the lower eye of each unit and a bolt passing through the centre of the bush secures the assembly to the axle casing. Two rubber washers are fitted on the upper end of the piston rod – one either side of the body member. Two steel washers are also fitted – one under the lower washer and one between the top washer and retaining nut. The two upper washers and retaining nut are visible on the body member at the front of the boot.

REAR SPRINGS

The rear springs are mounted on rubber bushes at the front and rear ends, so that no lubrication is called for at these points.

Every 5,000 miles, the spring leaves should be brushed clean and sprayed with penetrating oil. This operation is best carried out with the car jacked up at the normal jacking points, so that the axle is hanging and the springs leaves will tend to open up to ensure better lubrication. After lubricating the springs, lower the car to the ground and check the tightness of the rear-spring U-bolts. Do not use excessive leverage on these nuts; a normal spanner is sufficient.

SUSPENSION TROUBLES AND REMEDIES

Provided the shock-absorber fluid level is correct, little trouble will be experienced from them. A weak or faulty shock absorber will allow the car to bounce excessively and if this condition is experienced, the unit should be overhauled or replaced.

If the mounting bolts are loose, or the rubber mountings of the shock absorbers are worn, this will cause knocking and should be checked and renewed if necessary.

Worn rear-spring bushes may give rise to a knocking on rough surfaces. This can be checked by inserting a suitable lever between the front-spring eye and its mounting bracket and checking for movement at this point. The rear-shackle bushes and radius-arm bushes (where fitted) can be checked in a similar manner and, if there is movement, the bushes should be renewed.

Never attempt to remove the front-suspension unit, as the coil spring must be clamped in its normal laden position. Any attempt to remove the unit without clamping the spring may be very dangerous.

Chapter 12

BRAKING SYSTEM

ALL models of the Consul Corsair are fitted with disc brakes on the front wheels and leading- and trailing-shoe drum brakes on the rear wheels; G.T. cars are fitted with a vacuum-assisted hydraulic servo. The hand-brake lever is mounted under the instrument panel and is connected through a relay lever in the engine compartment to a flexible cable and conduit. The cable conduit is retained in a flexibly mounted equalizer, the cable being connected directly to the left-hand rear-brake plate; a rod connects the equalizer bracket to the right-hand rear-brake plate. As the hand-brake is applied, the cable pulls directly on the left-hand expander and the reaction of the conduit on the equalizer applies the right-hand brake by the transverse rod.

Although the front disc brakes are self-adjusting, the rear-brake shoes should be adjusted at the regular service periods.

The pendant brake pedal is located on a bracket secured to the engine-compartment bulkhead and connected by a short push-rod to the combined master cylinder and brake-fluid reservoir in the engine compartment.

On Standard and De Luxe models, the master cylinder is connected to a four-way union, separate pipes from this union connecting to flexible pipes fitted to the front-brake calipers. Another pipe from the four-way union connects to a flexible pipe at the rear axle; the other end of the flexible pipe is connected to the right-hand rear-wheel cylinder. A transfer pipe across the axle connects the right-hand and left-hand rear-wheel cylinders. Bleed valves are fitted on each front-brake caliper and on the left-hand rear-wheel cylinder. A mechanically-operated stop-lamp switch is fitted on the brake-pedal bracket. On G.T. models, the master cylinder is connected to the servo unit, which transfers fluid at increased pressure to the four-way union and pipes as on Standard and De Luxe models.

MAINTENANCE SCHEDULE

The brake-fluid level in the reservoir should be checked weekly, at the first 500-mile service and at each 5,000-mile service.

The rear-brake shoes should be adjusted at the first 500-mile service, and inspected and adjusted at each 5,000-mile service.

The condition of the front-brake pads should also be checked at each 5,000-mile service.

No lubrication is called for on the main hand-brake cable as the cable conduit is pre-packed with grease. However, the relay-lever fulcrum and primary cable should be lubricated with engine oil every 5,000 miles.

The brake pedal should feel firm under all conditions. If the pedal feels spongy, this is an indication that air has got into the hydraulic braking system and the system must be bled to eliminate this air. Do not confuse a spongy pedal with excess pedal travel.

Due to the self-adjusting characteristics of the front disc brakes, increase in brake-pedal travel is due to wear on the rear-brake shoes. This will not increase as much as on a fully drum-braked car. Some guide to rear-brake shoe condition can be obtained by checking the handbrake travel. If the handbrake is hard on after moving through six notches when correctly adjusted, it may be found that shoe adjustment is required when the brake can be pulled out for ten notches.

Because of the limited increase in brake-pedal travel, the servicing and inspection periods should be adhered to, to prevent excessive lining wear which could result in damaged brake drums or discs.

Adding Fluid to
Master-cylinder Reservoir

The hydraulic brake-fluid reservoir is incorporated in the brake master cylinder and is mounted on the engine bulkhead alongside the clutch master cylinder and reservoir. At the above periods, the hydraulic fluid level should be checked. The fluid level is marked on the outside of the reservoir; this being approximately $\frac{5}{8}$ in. below the top of the container.

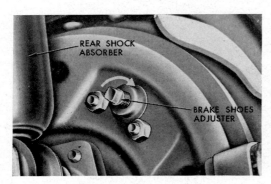

Before removing the reservoir cap to check the fluid level, wipe the reservoir and cap with a piece of clean rag to eliminate the possibility of any dirt entering the system. Use only clean rag for this, do not use a rag that has been soaked in petrol or paraffin as, if this contacts the fluid, the seals in the master cylinder and wheel cylinders will be damaged.

Unscrew the reservoir cap and check the fluid level. If this is below the line marked on the outside of the casing, add sufficient fluid to bring it up to the correct level. Before refitting the reservoir cap, check that the vent hole in the cap is clear, then refit the cap.

When topping up the brake and clutch master-cylinder reservoirs, use only the correct type of brake fluid which is serviced under its Part No. ME3833E. Use only a clean container for brake fluid as if this is contaminated with mineral oil of any kind, the master-cylinder and wheel-cylinder seals will be damaged making the brake and clutch mechanism inoperative. The whole system will then have to be thoroughly cleaned out and the seals renewed. Take care not to spill brake fluid on the paintwork or this may be damaged.

An illustration showing the clutch- and brake-fluid reservoirs is given on page 52.

Checking for Leaks

If it is constantly necessary to add brake fluid to the reservoir, this is a definite sign of leaks either at the master cylinder or in the pipe lines and unions. Thoroughly clean off all union nuts and check for signs of brake-fluid leakage at these points. If any doubt exists, get someone

49. ADJUSTING REAR-WHEEL DRUM BRAKES

A threaded square-headed adjuster is fitted on the backplate of each rear brake and is located forward and above the rear-axle casing (diametrically opposite the expander unit).

To adjust the rear brakes, first ensure that the brake drums are cold, jack up the rear wheels and release the handbrake.

Screw in the adjuster clockwise until the brake drum is locked. Then unscrew the adjuster (anti-clockwise) approximately two clicks until brake drum turns freely. Adjust the other rear brake in a similar manner.

to press the brake pedal down hard whilst the unions and pipes are inspected for leakage. Occasionally examine the flexible pipes connecting each front-brake caliper to its supply pipe and the flexible pipe located over the rear axle connecting the rear brakes to the rear-supply pipe.

Handbrake-linkage Lubrication

The only lubrication required on the brake linkage is on the relay-lever fulcrum and primary cable. The footbrake pedal is mounted on pre-lubricated bushes, whilst the main handbrake cable operates through a pre-packed conduit.

The handbrake relay-lever fulcrum and primary cable should be lubricated with engine oil at the first 500-mile service and every 5,000-mile service. At the same time, a few drops of oil can be put on other clevises in the linkage to prevent wear and possible seizure at these points.

Rear-brake Adjustment and
Brake-shoe Inspection

At the first 500-mile service and whenever the handbrake travel becomes excessive, the rear brakes should be adjusted. Every 5,000 miles, the brake shoes and pads should be inspected for wear and the rear brakes re-adjusted at the same time.

The rear-brake shoe adjuster on each back-plate is located forward and above the rear-axle casing and is a square-headed unit. To adjust the rear brakes, jack up the car, release the handbrake and screw in the square-headed adjuster (clockwise) until the brake drum is locked. Then screw out the adjuster (anti-clockwise) approximately two clicks until the drum turns freely.

Handbrake Adjustment

Normally, adjustment of the rear-brake shoes will automatically adjust the handbrake linkage. If the handbrake-lever travel is excessive and the rear-brake shoe adjustment is correct, the handbrake linkage should be adjusted.

To adjust the handbrake linkage, jack up the vehicle and lock the brake drums with the square-headed adjuster located above and forward of the rear axle. Pull the rubber gaiter away from the equalizer on the rear-axle casing to expose the locknut on the handbrake cable-conduit sleeve and slacken this nut. At the same time, slacken the two nuts securing the trans-verse pull-rod to the equalizer. Tighten the adjusting nut on the conduit sleeve until all play is taken out of the brake cable. Adjust the two nuts on the transverse rod to set the equalizer at right angles to the rear-axle casing. Then tighten the nuts, taking care not to alter the setting of the equalizer and finally tighten the adjusting-sleeve locknut and refit the rubber gaiter.

Release the adjusters on the brake back-plates two clicks, so that the drums are free. The handbrake lever should now move through six to seven notches to lock the rear wheels. There is no adjustment on the handbrake primary cable.

Rear-brake Shoe Inspection and Replacement

Every 5,000 miles, the rear-brake drums should be removed and the brake linings inspected for wear. The brake linings should not be worn to within less than $\frac{1}{32}$ in. above the heads of the rivets. If the lining is thinner than this the shoes must be renewed. At the same time, inspect the wheel cylinders for fluid leaks; if any leaks are apparent, the seals must be renewed.

To remove the rear-brake shoes, first jack up

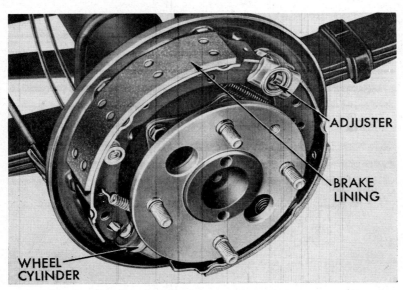

50. ARRANGEMENT OF REAR-BRAKE SHOE ASSEMBLY ON ALL MODELS

the car, remove the road wheels and release the handbrake. The brake drum is retained to the axle-shaft flange by a countersunk screw – remove the screw and pull off the brake drum.

The brake shoes are held in contact with the backplate by a retaining clip which locates on a spindle passing through the backplate and shoe web. Depress the retaining clip to release it from the spindle and pull the spindle from the backplate. Lift each shoe out of engagement with the adjuster tappets, and detach the other end of the shoes from the wheel-cylinder piston. Remove the shoes and detach the springs. Note that the symmetrical spring is fitted between

is not so, the tappets have been interchanged and the assembly should be reversed.

Before assembling the new brake shoes, note the difference in the shape of the ends of the shoe webs. The squared end locates in the adjuster tappets and the other, curved end, locates in the wheel-cylinder piston. The shoe linings are not symmetrical, the leading edge of each shoe being unlined.

To assemble the shoes to the brake backplate, fit the upper shoe in position with the leading (unlined end) and the curved end of the web in the wheel-cylinder piston, and the other end in the adjuster. Hook one end of the symmetrical

51. FRONT DISC PAD RENEWAL (1)
1. Retaining pins.
2. Caliper.
3. Retaining-pin clips.

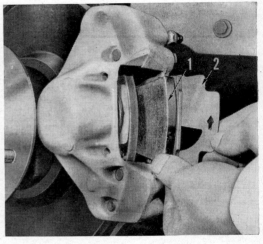

52. FRONT DISC PAD RENEWAL (2)
1. Brake pad.
2. Shim.

the adjuster ends of the shoes. The other spring is fitted with the coiled end towards the upper shoe, the ends of the springs being located in the second hole in each shoe web. Do not depress the brake pedal when the shoes are detached or the wheel-cylinder pistons will be ejected.

Clean off the backplate, grease the shoe thrust pads on the plate with high-melting-point grease. Remove the tappets from the adjuster housing, clean and grease them, screw the adjuster fully anti-clockwise and refit the tappets. Check that when the tappets are held in contact with the adjuster cone, the slot for the shoe web is parallel to the backplate; if this

spring into the second hole in the shoe web at the adjuster end of the shoe, and hook the coiled end of the other spring into the second hole in the web at the wheel cylinder end. Attach the other shoe to the springs in the same locations, with the unlined and square end of the web towards the adjuster, and the lined end with the curved web towards the wheel cylinder. Hold the top shoe in position and locate the lower shoe in the expander tappet and wheel cylinder.

Pass one of the spindles through the backplate and upper shoe web and fit the retaining clip; repeat this for the lower shoe.

Refit the brake drum to the axle-shaft flange taking care to line up the countersunk hole in the drum with the tapped hole in the axle flange, fit the countersunk screw and tighten it securely. Refit the road wheel and adjust the brakes as described previously in this chapter. Repeat for the other rear brake and finally check the tightness of the wheelnuts after the car is lowered to the ground; then refit the hub caps.

FRONT DISC BRAKES

The front disc brakes are self-adjusting so that there is little increase in pedal travel as wear takes place. Because of this, the brake pads should be inspected for wear at the regular servicing periods to prevent damage to the discs.

Renewing Disc Pads

The disc pads should be checked for wear every 5,000 miles and if the friction material thickness is less than $\frac{1}{8}$ in., the pads should be renewed. These can be checked *in situ*, although

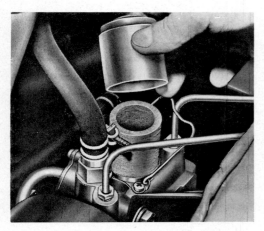

53. BRAKE-SERVO-UNIT AIR FILTER WITH COVER REMOVED

it may be helpful to remove the front wheels to do this.

If it is necessary to renew the brake pads, this operation can be done very simply. Jack up the car and remove the front wheels. Two retaining pins can be seen passing through two halves of the caliper assembly, these pins themselves being retained by a hairpin spring clip. Pull

out the spring clips and withdraw the retaining pins. The pads can now be pulled out of their location using a pair of thin-nosed pliers if necessary. Remove the shim fitted behind each pad. If the pads are being removed for inspection or whilst carrying out hub-bearing adjustment, note the position from which they are removed as they must be refitted, if not being renewed, in their original locations.

Before fitting the new pads inspect the cylinders for fluid leaks; if there are any leaks, the seals must be renewed. This is best done by your dealer. Similarly examine the discs to ensure they are not greasy; if they are greasy this may be due to damaged hub grease seals which again must be renewed (see Chapter 10 for hub and disc removal).

Wash both faces of the discs with petrol, ease the pistons back into their housings and slide the pads and shims into place. Take care that the pads are fitted with the friction face towards the brake disc, and the shims with the arrow pointing in the forward direction of rotation of the wheel. Clean off the retaining pins and slide them right home into the caliper; they should be an easy fit and should never be forced home. Once the pins are right home, fit the retaining clips. The straight leg on the clip should be pushed through the hole in the end of the pin, the other leg of the spring clip will then snap round the pin.

The lining material on the G.T. pads is different to that fitted on Standard and De Luxe models due to the higher braking pressures given by the vacuum servo – only the correct pads should be fitted to each model. The G.T. pads are identified by a green marking on the outer face of the pads, whilst the pads for use on Standard and De Luxe models have a red marking in this location. From December 1964, this is changed to red and yellow.

It is not necessary to bleed the brakes after renewing the pads but the pedal should be pumped several times until it becomes firm.

RENEWING SERVO-UNIT AIR FILTER (G.T. MODELS)

On G.T. cars there is one additional service point on the servo unit – the air filter, which should be renewed whenever the brake pads are replaced.

To renew the servo air filter, wipe the cover and surrounding area with a clean dry cloth, move the spring clip to one side and lift off the cover. The filter can now be lifted off its seat. Before fitting the new filter, clean the filter seat, then fit the filter and cover, securing the cover witn the wire clip.

CHECKING VACUUM-SERVO MOTOR (G.T. MODELS)

If the vacuum-servo motor becomes defective, the brake pedal action will be hard, requiring a high pressure to operate it which should be immediately apparent. The action of the servo can be checked in either one of two ways: (1) Run the engine for half a minute to exhaust the vacuum tank, then switch off. Pump the brake pedal on and off slowly and, each time it is applied, air should be heard being drawn into the servo. The noise will be more apparent with the bonnet open. (2) Operate the brake several times to fully exhaust the vacuum tank. Then apply the brake with a light pressure and start up the engine. As the vacuum is built up, the brake pedal will be drawn down under its influence. If the servo is thought to be faulty, it should be checked by your dealer.

BEDDING-IN OF BRAKE LININGS

After fitting new brake shoes or pads, the adjustment should be checked after 500 miles to compensate for the linings bedding-in. The brakes will not give the maximum efficiency until the linings are fully bedded-in. Always use the manufacturer's approved linings as these have been developed to give the best braking performance.

BLEEDING THE BRAKES

This operation is necessary to remove any air which may have got into the hydraulic brake fluid, e.g. when a pipe is disconnected or the level of the fluid in the master cylinder is allowed to get too low. The presence of air is indicated by the brake pedal having a spongy feel instead of the normal hard pressure felt when the brakes are applied. Do not confuse the excess pedal travel due to maladjusted brakes with the spongy feel of air in the system. To enable the brakes to be bled, a bleed valve fitted with a small rubber cap, and very similar in appearance to a grease nipple, is screwed into each front caliper and the left-hand rear-wheel cylinder.

When bleeding the brakes, work in the following sequence:
1. Right-hand front-wheel caliper
2. Other front-wheel caliper
3. Left-hand rear-wheel cylinder
4. Caliper bled first.

This is a two-handed job, one person operating the brake pedal and maintaining the fluid level in the master cylinder, the other doing the bleeding of the calipers and cylinder.

Remove the rubber cap from the bleed valve and fit a length of plastic or rubber pipe to the valve. Pour a quantity of fluid into a jar and immerse the free end of the pipe in this fluid; keep the end of the pipe below the surface of the fluid throughout the operation. Slacken the bleed valve (anticlockwise) half a turn and check that the master-cylinder fluid level is correct.

Press the brake pedal right down to the floor and quickly release it by sliding the foot off it, pause a few seconds to allow the master cylinder to recuperate and repeat the operation. As the pedal is depressed, fluid and/or air will be discharged from the tube, the air forming bubbles in the fluid in the jar. Continue pumping the brake pedal until all bubbling stops, indicating that all air has been removed from that portion of the system.

Once bubbling has stopped, depress the pedal once more and tighten the bleed valve whilst the pedal is held down. Release the pedal, remove the tube and refit the rubber dust cap to the bleed valve. Carry out this operation at all points in the above sequence.

Whilst carrying out this operation, it is important that the fluid in the master cylinder is maintained at the correct level; if this is allowed to get too low more air will be drawn into the system. Do not replenish the master cylinder with fluid that has been bled from the system as this will be heavily aerated, consequently air will be put back again.

Provided it is allowed to stand for a long time in a sealed container, fluid which has been bled out of the system can be added to the master cylinder when all the air has dispersed. Ideally, and for the quantity involved, the fluid should be thrown away and new fluid only used for topping up. Take care that brake fluid is not dropped on to the paintwork or it will damage it.

TESTING BRAKING SYSTEM

The efficiency of any braking system depends ultimately on the adhesion between the tyres and road surface. Before testing brake performance, inflate all tyres to the correct pressure and ensure that the tyres are evenly paired on each axle. If a good tyre is fitted on one side and a worn one on the other, or tyres of different makes with considerable variation in tread pattern, erratic braking performance will result. To check the brakes, drive on a good stretch of road, preferably dry and uncambered, and wherever possible choose a quiet road to avoid embarrassment to other traffic.

Before checking brake action at high speed, make two or three stops with a light pedal application from between 20 to 30 miles per hour to ensure that the performance is correct. The car should pull up squarely with no tendency to slew to one side or the other. Only when satisfied with the brakes at low speeds should a crash stop be attempted. Again, drive to 30 miles per hour and apply the footbrake pedal hard. The car should again pull up quite squarely. If necessary stops can be made from higher speeds provided the braking performance was satisfactory under the first tests.

Due to the automatic compensation given by hydraulic braking systems, even though one brake shoe may be binding slightly, there should normally be no tendency for the car to slew when braking. If this happens, it is an indication of some abnormal brake-lining condition and the linings should be inspected. If oil or grease is found on the brake linings, these should be renewed as it is practically impossible to get all the oil or grease out of the lining material and, due to heat generated during braking, this will be drawn up from the inside of the lining to the surface, again giving erratic performance.

The brakes can be checked for binding by driving and using the brakes as little as possible, finally allowing the car to coast to a stop. Feel each rear brake drum and if one is found to be much hotter than the others, it indicates that these brake shoes are binding and should be readjusted. Always slack off the shoes of the binding drum – never tighten the other shoes to cause binding on all drums.

It should be remembered that erratic braking performance may not be due to the braking system, but may be traced to the steering. Provided that the condition of the brake shoes, brake adjustment and tyres are correct, a check should be made on the steering. This, of course, will at the same time be noticed when driving the vehicle normally.

BRAKE SQUEAL

Brake squeal, although an annoying fault, is not detrimental. This is one of the most common brake faults and at the same time the most difficult to rectify. Squeal when applying the brakes first thing in the morning is quite normal, and is generally due to condensation and slight rust formation on the linings and brake drums or discs. After a few brake applications, when the system has been heated up, this normally disappears. If squeal is persistent, this may be due to excessive brake lining dust in the rear-brake drums. The brake drums should be removed and thoroughly cleaned out, at the same time blowing off any dust on the brake shoes. The surface of the brake linings can be lightly rubbed with fine sandpaper to remove any hard glazing which may have formed on the surface of the brake linings.

BRAKING SYSTEM SPECIFICATION

Front brakes

Disc diameter	..	..	9·5 in.
Pad lining area	..	..	17·94 sq. in. (total)
Pad identification:			
Standard and De Luxe	..		Red paint spot*
G.T.	..	..	Green paint spot

Rear Brakes

Drum diameter	..	..	9·00 in.
Lining width	..	..	1·75 in.
Lining area	..	..	57·60 sq. in.

* Red and yellow paint spot from December 1964.

Chapter 13

WHEELS AND TYRES

THE wide-base 13-in.-diameter pressed-steel wheels are mounted on the hubs on four studs and retained by right-hand-threaded nuts on both sides. Tubeless 5·60 × 13 tyres are fitted as standard equipment, white sidewall tyres being available as an optional fitment.

The tyre pressures should be checked weekly, when the tyres are cold, using an accurate pressure gauge. On Standard and De Luxe models these should be 22 lb/sq. in. (front and rear), whilst on G.T. models for normal driving these should be 24 lb/sq. in. (front) and 26 lb/sq. in (rear). On the G.T. models for sustained high-speed driving (speeds in excess of 80 m.p.h.), the tyre pressures should be increased by 4 lb/sq. in. all round to 28 lb/sq. in. (front) and 30 lb/sq. in (rear).

After the first 500 miles and after a similar mileage when a wheel has been refitted, the security of the wheel nuts should be checked.

When checking the tightness of the wheel nuts, lever off the chromium-plated hub cap and remove the trim ring (if fitted). Then, using the wheel brace supplied with the car, attempt to tighten each nut, remembering that all nuts are right-hand threaded and should be turned clockwise to tighten. Do not use excessive leverage when checking these nuts, the car wheel brace is all that is required.

Periodically examine the tyres and remove any flints or stones which have become embedded in the tyre treads – this can be done at each 5,000-mile service when carrying out the brake adjustments.

WHEEL CHANGING

To change a wheel, stand the car on level ground and apply the handbrake securely. If this has to be done in an emergency, with the car standing on a hill and one of the rear wheels

has to be removed, it is advisable to position a block against the front wheels to prevent possible movement. If no block is available, the front wheels should be turned so that the kerb will act as a block. Remove the hub cap, slacken each wheel nut half a turn and remove the spare wheel from its well in the luggage boot

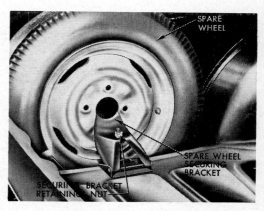

54. SPARE WHEEL LOCATION IN LUGGAGE BOOT

before jacking up the car. The spare wheel is housed in a well on the left-hand side of the luggage boot and is retained by a clamp secured to the boot floor. Unscrew the clamping nut sufficiently to allow the bolt to swivel out of the clamp, which can then be swivelled out of the centre of the spare wheel.

Two jacking points are fitted on each side of the car. These are located in the lower face of the rocker panels behind each front wheel and just in front of each rear wheel. The jacking points have a hole in them to accommodate the conical end of the jack arm. To operate the jack, fit the handle on the square shank of the screws with the words 'To Raise' outwards. Lay

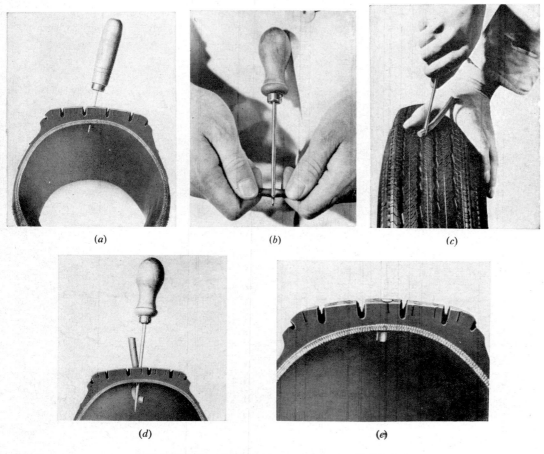

(a)   (b)   (c)

(d)   (e)

55. TEMPORARY REPAIR OF TUBELESS TYRES

Tubeless tyres need not be removed from the wheel in order to temporarily repair a simple puncture. The accompanying illustrations show the procedure using the Dunlop Reddiplug repair kit. Never use more than one plug per hole.

Do not use rubber plugs for sidewall repairs to cross-ply or radial-ply tyres.

For radial-ply tyre repairs, the Reddiplug method should not be used in the tread area extending 1⅛ in. inwards from the outer edge of the tread in contact with the road.

Where a rubber plug repair has been carried out, the earliest opportunity should be taken to get a cold patch or a properly vulcanized repair made.

(a) Insert the wire probe through hole to find direction of the penetration. Leave probe in position on a cross-ply type. On a radial-ply tyre remove wire probe and insert rasp (supplied with kit) through hole in anti-clockwise direction and leave in position. *Do not work rasp up and down in cover.*

Coat plugging tool with rubber solution, remove wire probe (or rasp) and insert plugging tool through hole; work tool up and down to lubricate the hole. Repeat this operation until the hole is well lubricated.

(b) Stretch and roll rubber plug into eye of plugging tool about ¼ in. from end of plug.

(c) Dip plug and plugging tool into rubber solution and insert into hole.

(d) It is necessary to push the rubber plug right through the casing as shown.

(e) When the plugging tool is withdrawn, trim off the rubber plug level with tread and inflate the tyre.

the jack on the ground and operate the handle to and fro to raise the jack arm so that its conical head enters the hole in the jacking member. Ensure that the arm is correctly located in the hole in the member before fully lifting the car. Jack up until the wheel is well

56. IRREGULAR (SPOTTY) FRONT-TYRE WEAR

The nature of spotty wear on front tyres indicates an alternating 'slip grip' phenomenon, but it is seldom possible to associate its origin and development with any single cause.

Corrections which may follow a check of the following possible causes will not always effect a complete cure and it may be necessary to interchange wheel positions and reverse directions of rotation at suitable intervals.

A number of causes of spotty wear on front tyres are: wrong inflation pressures, brake binding, brake unbalance, condition of brake drum, incorrect wheel alignment, play in hub bearings, suspension bearings and steering joints. Bad wheel concentricity at tyre-bead seats, faulty road springs, shock absorbers and unbalanced tyre and wheel assemblies.

Note. It is now an offence if a tyre does not have a tread pattern at least 1mm. deep in a continuous band of pattern at least three-quarters of the tread width. It is also an offence if the tyre is unsuitable either in itself or in combination with other tyres on the vehicle; not properly inflated; or has a break in its fabric or a serious cut, a lump or bulge caused by ply separation or failure, or any portion of the ply structure exposed.

clear of the ground, then unscrew the wheel nuts and lift off the wheel.

Fit the spare wheel and screw on the wheel nuts, conical end first. Then screw up the nuts to grip the wheel, tightening each one a few turns at a time, working diametrically across the wheel to seat the wheel evenly. When all the wheel nuts are tight, reverse the jack handle on the shaft and lower the car to the ground. Finally, tighten all nuts before refitting the hub cap.

If a wheel has to be changed in wet weather, remove the rubber plug from the base of the

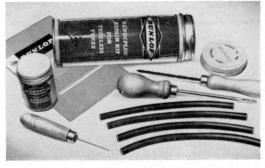

57. DUNLOP REDDIPLUG REPAIR KIT FOR THE TEMPORARY REPAIR OF SIMPLE PUNCTURES IN TUBELESS TYRES

spare-wheel well before putting the punctured wheel back in the luggage boot, so that the water can drain off the wheel and out of the well.

Fit the spare wheel in the well and swivel the clamp inwards so that it locates in the centre of the wheel. Swing the bolt into the slot in the clamp and tighten the nut to retain the clamp in position.

To obtain maximum tyre life, it will be found helpful to reposition the wheels on the car every 5,000 miles. It should be remembered, however, that if the wheels have been balanced on the car they may have to be re-balanced after they have been changed round.

If every 5,000 miles, the wheels are changed round to even out tyre wear, they should be re-positioned as follows:

Spare wheel to near-side front,
near-side front to near-side rear,
near-side rear to off-side front,
off-side front to off-side rear and,
off-side rear to spare wheel.

If, for any reason, the spare wheel is not brought into rotation, the wheels should be transferred diagonally, that is, near-side front to off-side rear, off-side front to near-side rear and vice versa.

IMPORTANCE OF CORRECT TYRE PRESSURES

The tyre pressures should be checked weekly. Do not forget to check the spare wheel at the same time. Incorrect or uneven tyre pressures, apart from affecting the steering, brakes and general performance of the car, will reduce the tyre life considerably. Under-inflated tyres may cause the steering or brakes to pull to one side, but principally this will cause excessive flexing of the tyre walls, weakening these and considerably shortening the life of the tyre. Over-inflation will give a harsh ride and give increased wear in the centre of the tyre.

If, on checking tyre pressures, it is found that one tyre consistently loses pressure, the reason for this should be determined. First check that the valve core is screwed right home; if this is tight, check that the valve is air-tight. This can be done by holding an egg-cup full of water, so that the end of the valve is immersed in the water; any leak will be indicated by bubbles in the water. If the valve is leaking, this may be due to dirt on the seat and this can sometimes be cleared by pressing down the valve spindle and allowing it to snap back on to its seat. If this does not rectify the trouble, a new valve core should be fitted. Valve caps are fitted to all valves to prevent dirt getting into the valve and these should, therefore, be replaced if any become lost.

INFLATING TUBELESS TYRES

When tubeless tyres have been completely deflated, it is essential that the beads are seated against the rim flanges to make an air-tight joint before re-inflating them. This calls for a supply of compressed air, so that if it is found that the valve cores are leaking these should be renewed by a garage, as it will be found impossible to inflate the tyre with a hand or foot pump.

TUBELESS TYRE REPAIRS

Simple punctures in tubeless tyres caused by nails, etc. can usually be temporarily repaired without removing the wheel from the car by using an appropriate tyre-repair kit.

It is the opinion of the tyre manufacturers that a single plug repair is merely a temporary expedient which the motorist himself can carry out provided he follows precisely the instructions on the repair kit; *such a repair must be made permanent by the addition of a cold patch or a properly vulcanized repair as soon as possible afterwards.*

As stated previously, if tubeless tyres have been completely deflated it is essential to have a supply of compressed air to re-inflate them and this job should only be carried out by a garage.

CAUSES OF EXCESSIVE TYRE WEAR

Uneven or excessive tyre wear on the front wheels is generally an indication of steering misalignment and this should be checked if this condition is found. Incorrect toe-in is generally indicated by flats worn on the inner or outer edges of the tyre. Where the tyre tread is scooped out around the centre of the tread, this may be an indication of incorrect wheel-bearing adjustment. Normally, it will be found that the rear tyres wear evenly but if, however, it is found that one wears more rapidly than the other, this may be an indication that the rear axle is misaligned, due to loose spring U-bolts or a broken spring centre bolt and, again, this condition should be checked.

Chapter 14

BODYWORK UPKEEP

THE pressed-steel integral-construction body calls for little maintenance apart from regular cleaning to maintain its good appearance. The car should always be washed, never dry cleaned, as this will scratch the surface of the paintwork and impair the high-gloss finish.

WASHING AND POLISHING

The ideal way of washing the car is with a pressure hose, as this ensures an ample supply of clean water to remove all road dirt and also enables the wheel arches and under-body of the car to be thoroughly cleaned. When using a pressure hose never turn the full force of the water on to the body as this will tend to force dirt into the paint. First of all, using low pressure, really well soak the car to soften and loosen the road dirt then, still using low pressure, sponge the body to remove all the dirt. Finally, well hose off the body before drying with a good chamois leather.

The use of a car shampoo will help to remove traffic film deposits which collect on the vehicle. The car should be sponged off with this solution after well soaking it to loosen and soften the road dirt. Finally, wash off the body and well dry it with a chamois leather.

If the car is washed and leathered regularly, the paint and bright metal finish will be kept in good condition. The use of a good-quality car polish occasionally will restore the original high lustre to the paintwork.

The head- and rear-lamp bezels, radiator grille, the roof-panel to rear-quarter panel mouldings and wheel-trim rings when fitted, are made of anodized aluminium; their surface finish can be retained by washing and polishing with car-body polish. Do not use a chrome cleaner on these parts or the gloss surface finish may be removed. Other bright metal parts can be safely polished with chrome cleaner.

In winter months, when salt has been put on the roads to prevent freezing, the car should be washed as soon as possible after completing a journey. If these salt solutions are allowed to dry on the car, they will cause corrosion, particularly of the bright metal parts. Similarly, if the car has been splashed with sea water it again should be washed as soon as possible to prevent corrosion by salt deposits. Occasionally, when washing the car, make sure that all mud and dirt are washed from around the jacking brackets or you may find that when the jack has to be used in an emergency, these holes are blocked, so making it difficult to fit the jack.

The use of a chrome protector will help to preserve the bright metal parts, particularly if the car is not kept in a garage. Before applying this, thoroughly clean the bright metal, removing all traces of corrosion, then apply the protector evenly and thinly. If care is taken in applying this, it will be practically indistinguishable. All corrosion should be removed before applying the protector or otherwise this may tend to spread under it.

UPHOLSTERY

The interior, seats, head lining, etc., can be cleaned as required with any good-quality upholstery cleaner. Alternatively, the interior may be cleaned with a damp cloth and toilet soap. After removing all the dirt, again wipe over the area with a damp cloth, finally wiping dry and polishing with a clean soft cloth. Never use any form of polish on the upholstery; rubbing with a soft cloth is all that is necessary.

LUBRICATION OF DOOR LOCKS AND HINGES

Occasionally, the door hinges and locks, etc., should be lubricated to keep them free in operation. Apply a few drops of penetrating oil to the hinges or lock mechanisms, taking care to wipe off all surplus oil to prevent damage to clothing. Apply one or two drops of very light oil to the sides of the door key, and insert the key in the lock two or three times as this will help to lubricate the internal mechanism of the lock. Do not over-lubricate or use heavy oil at this point, as this may help dust to collect internally, so eventually jamming the lock. In winter months, if it is found impossible to turn the key, due to the lock having frozen internally, warm the key for a few seconds in a flame before fitting it to the lock; this will normally thaw out the lock and allow the key to turn.

Drain holes are provided in the bottom edge of each door to allow surplus water, which may get inside the door, to run away. Occasionally, probe these holes with a piece of wire to make sure they are unobstructed so that any water can run out of the inside of the door, so preventing internal corrosion.

DOOR STRIKER-PLATE ADJUSTMENT

After a while rattles may develop from the doors due to slight wear on the door lock and striker mechanism. To check for this, close the door and push and pull on the handle. If there is movement present, it indicates that the striker plates should be adjusted. Slacken the screws retaining the striker plate and move it slightly inwards, re-tightening the screws afterwards. Again, check for movement of the door; if this is still present, the striker plate needs to be moved farther inwards. If the door is difficult to close, the striker plate has been moved too far and should be moved outwards slightly to give an easy door shut but just sufficient to eliminate movement when the door is closed.

Occasionally check the tightness of all screws, seat-mounting bracket bolts, etc., to prevent rattles developing.

TOUCHING-UP PAINTWORK

Any paint chips or scratches should be touched up as soon as possible to prevent rust developing and affecting a much greater area. For this purpose a touch-up kit of the appropriate body colour can be obtained from any Ford Dealer and is a very worthwhile accessory. Any dents or dings that may have occurred should be left to the professional to knock out, as this can often be done without damaging the paintwork.

Tar stains on the paintwork can be removed by rubbing with a soft cloth moistened with a mixture of two-thirds petrol and one-third clean engine oil. After the stain has been removed, wash the body and lightly polish the affected area.

F

Chapter 15

ELECTRICAL SYSTEM

A TWELVE-VOLT, positive-earth electrical system is used, the battery being located on the right-hand side of the engine compartment. The generator mounted on the left-hand side of the engine is driven in tandem with the water pump by a V-belt from the crankshaft pulley. The generator is a two-brush machine, the charging rate being controlled by a combined voltage- and current-control regulator located on the engine side panel.

No fuses are incorporated in the main electrical circuit, although a 5-amp fuse is fitted in the direction-indicator circuit and is contained in a bayonet-type plastic holder fitted in the feed wire located behind the instrument panel. An earth strap is connected between the gearbox and floor pan of the car on the right-hand side.

The wiring diagrams on pages 90 and 91 illustrate the electrical system and its associated components.

The electrolyte level of the battery should be checked every week and the generator rear bearing lubricated every 5,000 miles.

BATTERY MAINTENANCE

The twelve-volt lead acid battery has its positive terminal connected to earth on the engine compartment. The battery is of 38-ampere-hour capacity, although a larger battery of 51-ampere-hour capacity may be fitted.

The battery is the heart of the electrical system and to obtain the maximum efficiency from all the electrical components, the battery must be kept in good condition.

Adding Distilled Water

Every week remove the filler plugs from the battery top and check the level of the electrolyte – this should be $\frac{1}{4}$ in. above the top of the separators. If necessary, add distilled water to bring the electrolyte to this level. Never add anything to the battery except clean distilled water, which should always be stored in a glass container. It should never be necessary to add acid to a battery unless this has been lost through spillage; if this has occurred, acid should only be added by a responsible electrician.

In very cold weather, only add distilled water to the battery before running the engine. This will allow the water to mix completely with the electrolyte, otherwise the distilled water will

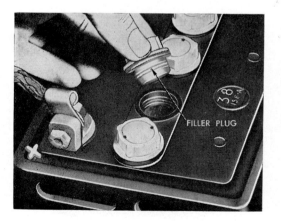

58. SHOWING ONE OF THE FILLER PLUGS REMOVED FROM BATTERY

The electrolyte level in each cell should be kept to $\frac{1}{4}$–$\frac{3}{8}$ in. above the top of the separators, by topping up with distilled water.

Check the level every week and top up as required.

not mix and may freeze, causing damage to the battery casing. After topping up the battery, replace the filler plugs and wipe the plugs and battery top.

Cleaning Battery Connections

The battery top must be kept clean and dry and any spillage should be wiped off with a cloth moistened with ammonia to neutralize the acid. If there are any signs of cracking around the cell lids, these should be resealed to prevent acid spillage and corrosion. The battery should be kept firmly clamped in its holder but, at the same time, care should be taken not to over-tighten the clamp to prevent damage to the battery casing.

A check should be made on the battery terminals to ensure that they are tight; if corrosion occurs on the terminals, this should be thoroughly cleaned off. It may be found best to remove the battery to carry out this operation, so that any corrosion on the battery terminals can be removed as well as corrosion on the cable terminals. To do this disconnect both cables from the battery posts, unscrew and remove the nut, flat washer and clamp-retaining bolt and remove the clamp from the battery carrier. Slide the battery rearwards so that the lug on the base disengages the front clamp and lift out the battery.

Remove any corrosion from around the battery post, and scrape it to make a clean connection at this point. Similarly, scrape all corrosion from the cable terminals and wipe both the cable terminals and posts with a rag moistened with ammonia. If necessary, the battery earth strap can be disconnected from the body and the mating faces of the earth strap and body thoroughly cleaned to give a good connection at this point. Any corrosion which may have occurred on the battery carrier should also be cleaned off, afterwards wiping it with a rag moistened with ammonia and repainting to prevent further corrosion.

Refit the battery, with the terminals towards the side of the engine compartment. Locate the lug on the base of the battery under the front clamp, then fit the rear clamp, bolt, flat washer and nut, tightening the nut just sufficiently to retain the battery. Do not overtighten the nut

or this may damage the battery case. Refit the cables – although the battery cannot be fitted wrongly – it should be remembered that the battery positive terminal is connected to earth, that is, to the body of the car. This terminal is marked with a $+$ sign and its base is coloured red. After reconnecting the terminals, coat them with petroleum jelly to reduce further corrosion. Never use grease for this, as this may melt under the engine heat, and soften the sealer around the cell lids.

Specific Gravity of Electrolyte

The battery should normally be maintained in a good state of charge by the current-voltage control regulator, which automatically adjusts the charging rate as necessary. If the battery is low in charge, the charging rate will be high and gradually reduced as the battery charge increases. The state of charge of the battery can be checked by using a hydrometer to check the specific gravity of the electrolyte.

For a fully-charged battery, the specific gravity should be 1·270 to 1·285 at 70° F.; corrections should be made to this reading for any variation in temperature by adding 0·004 to the reading for each 10° above 70° F. or subtracting 0·004 from the reading for each 10° below 70° F. If it is found that the specific gravity reading does not come within this range, even after a long run, or if the battery is using a large amount of distilled water, the charging system must be checked.

Battery Recharging

If at any time the battery has become discharged, it is advisable to remove it from the car to recharge it completely. Recharging the battery, particularly if it has been in service for a long time, should be done slowly to prevent overheating and possible internal damage.

Where the car is not used much during the winter months, a trickle charger may be used with advantage to keep the battery in a fully-charged condition.

Should it be necessary to lay up the car at any time, the battery should be removed from the car and fully charged before being stored. This will prevent the battery freezing in winter months and damaging the casing but, if possible, it is preferable to store the battery indoors rather than in an unheated garage. Even though not in use, a battery will gradually discharge itself and the state of charge should be checked monthly and the battery recharged if necessary.

GENERATOR

The generator is a two-brush machine and is driven at one and a half times the engine speed. A current-voltage control regulator adjusts the charging rate in accordance with the state of charge of the battery. A high-charging rate is given when the battery is low in charge, this reducing to a trickle charge as the battery becomes fully charged. No ammeter is fitted in the charging circuit (except on G.T. models) but a generator warning light is incorporated in the instrument panel.

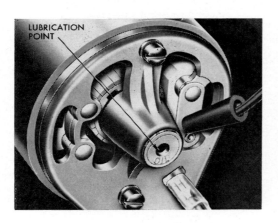

LUBRICATION POINT

Generator Warning Light

The generator-warning light is coloured red and marked GEN and will light when the ignition is switched on and the generator not charging, the light going out as the generator starts to charge the battery. If, at any time, the light does not come on when the ignition is switched on, the bulb should be removed and checked. If the bulb is satisfactory, the wiring to the bulb should be checked for breaks. Similarly, if the light does not go out as the engine speed increases, the charging circuit, that is, the generator and regulator, should be checked, as this indicates that the battery is not being charged.

Fan Belt Adjustment

The fan-belt tension should be checked every 5,000 miles by pushing and pulling on the fan belt at a point half-way between the generator and fan pulleys. The total free movement at this point should be $\frac{1}{2}$ in. If the fan-belt tension is too slack, slipping will occur which may cause wear on the fan belt and pulleys. At the same time, a slack belt could give an erratic charging rate, or possibly no charge at all, and may cause engine overheating. If the fan-belt tension is too tight, the generator and water-pump bearings may be overloaded, so giving short life to these bearings.

If the fan-belt tension is incorrect, slacken the two bolts securing the generator to the mounting brackets on the cylinder block, and the one bolt securing the generator to the

59. LUBRICATION OF GENERATOR REAR BEARING

The bronze-bush rear bearing of the generator should be lubricated every 5,000 miles by adding two drops of engine oil through lubrication hole.

Avoid excessive lubrication to prevent possibility of oil reaching the commutator and generator brushes so affecting the charging rate of the generator.

The front ball-bearing of the generator is pre-packed with grease and no lubrication is required.

adjusting strap. Swivel the generator on its mounting brackets until the correct fan-belt tension is obtained and securely tighten all three bolts.

Generator Rear-bearing Lubrication

The front bearing of the generator is a pre-packed ball bearing and no lubrication is required at this point. The rear bearing of the generator is a bronze bush and this should be lubricated every 5,000 miles by adding two drops of engine oil through the lubrication hole in the centre of the end plate. Do not over-lubricate this point, as excess oil may reach the armature commutator and generator brushes, so affecting the charging rate.

Cleaning Generator Commutator

The armature commutator is visible through one of the holes in the end plate and, if this is dirty or burnt, it may cause a poor charging rate and should, therefore, be cleaned. To do this it is necessary to remove the generator from the engine. Disconnect the two leads from the terminals on the end plate, noting that the thicker lead with a yellow tracer is connected to the larger terminal. Remove the bolt securing the generator to the adjusting strap and slacken the two bolts securing the generator to its mounting brackets. Move the generator inwards as far as possible and lift off the fan belt. Finally, remove the two bolts securing the generator to the mounting bracket and lift out the generator.

Unscrew the through bolts and withdraw them, when the end plate can be removed. The armature complete with the front plate can now be removed from the generator carcase, taking care not to lose the fibre washer fitted on the end of the armature shaft.

If the commutator is dirty, this may be cleaned with a petrol-moistened rag or very fine glass paper. If the commutator is badly burnt it will have to be skimmed to restore the surface and, at the same time, the insulation between the commutator segments cut down. This operation should normally be left to a competent electrician.

Generator Brushgear

At the same time as the commutator is being inspected, the two brushes secured to the end plate should be checked for free movement in their holders; if they are sticking, the edges of the brushes can be eased slightly to prevent this. The normal length of the brushes is 0·71 in. and, if they are worn excessively below this dimension, they should be renewed, as the springs cannot maintain the correct tension required by the brushes. To renew the brushes, lift up the springs and withdraw the brushes from their holders. Unscrew the screws securing the brush leads to their holders. The new brush leads should be secured to the holders and the brushes fitted into the holders, checking that they move quite freely.

Reassembling Generator

To reassemble the generator, install the armature and front end-plate assembly in the generator yoke, taking care that the mating marks are correctly aligned. Ease the brushes back in their holders against the spring tension, so that they can slide on to the surface of the commutator and install the rear end plate, again checking the mating marks. Fit and securely tighten the two through bolts.

The generator can now be located on its brackets, loosely fitting the two bolts and nuts securing it. Move the generator fully inwards and refit the fan belt. Refit the nut and bolt securing the adjusting strap to the front face of the end plate, then pull the generator outwards to get the correct fan-belt tension and tighten the three bolts and nuts securely. Reconnect the leads to the terminals, making sure that the thicker lead with a yellow tracer is connected to the larger terminal.

STARTER MOTOR

The solenoid-operated starter motor is mounted on the right-hand side of the engine. The solenoid is controlled by a separate switch incorporated in the ignition switch. When the ignition key is turned to the fully right position, the solenoid is energized, so completing the circuit and operating the starter motor. If at any time this switch appears to be faulty, a check can be made (except on cars fitted with automatic transmission) by depressing the rubber plunger in the centre of the solenoid switch which is mounted just behind the battery. This will close the solenoid contacts mechanically and, if the starter motor now operates, will indicate either a faulty solenoid, ignition switch or wiring. Before carrying out this test always ensure that the car is in neutral.

On cars fitted with automatic transmission, the solenoid plunger is covered with a metal cap to prevent the engine being inadvertently started when 'D' is selected and this test cannot be carried out.

Cleaning Starter-motor Connections

The starter motor draws a very high current from the battery and any loose or dirty connections in the starter-motor circuit will have a marked affect on its performance, giving a reduced cranking speed. Occasionally check the security and cleanliness of all connections in the starter circuit, that is, the two terminals on the solenoid switch, the terminal on the starter end plate, the connections on the earth strap between the gearbox and body frame and the battery terminals themselves. Before checking the connections on the solenoid and starter motor, always disconnect the battery positive terminal to prevent accidentally causing short circuits.

Provided that the battery is fully charged, and all connections clean and tight, a slow cranking speed may be due to a dirty commutator on the starter armature. If this is so, the starter motor can be removed and the commutator and brushes checked in a similar manner to the generator described previously. The starter-motor pinion is mounted on a screwed sleeve and whilst the starter motor is removed, this sleeve should be checked for oil or grease. If the sleeve is found to be greasy, it should be well washed with petrol as this may prevent the pinion engaging with the flywheel ring gear when the starter switch is operated.

Freeing Jammed Starter-motor Pinion

If the starter pinion becomes jammed with the flywheel ring gear, so that the starter does not operate when switched on, this can be released after removing the end cap located in the centre of the starter end plate and rotating the squared end of the armature shaft with a suitable spanner. Do not use excessive leverage when attempting to free a jammed starter as this may bend the armature shaft. Similarly, if the starter motor jams frequently, it is an indication of a worn flywheel ring gear or a bent starter-motor armature shaft and these components should be checked for their condition.

LIGHTING SYSTEM BULBS

Twelve-volt bulbs are fitted throughout, the wattage being as follows:

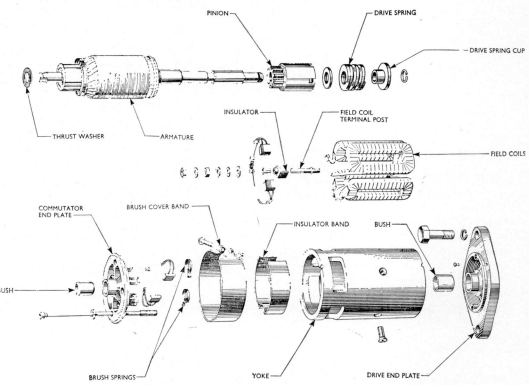

60. EXPLODED VIEW OF STARTER MOTOR

Bulb				Wattage
Headlamp sealed-beam units	..		..	60/45
Sidelamp bulbs	..	..	..	6
Rear and stop-lamp bulbs	..	..	..	6/24
Front and rear-direction indicator bulbs			..	24
Interior lamp bulb	..	..	..	6
Rear number-plate lamp bulb	..	..	..	6
All warning lights and instrument-panel bulbs	..	..	..	2·2

RENEWING SEALED-BEAM HEADLAMP UNIT

The headlamps are fully-sealed beam units, the light filaments being sealed into the reflector so that the lens and reflector form the

on the back of the reflector, the new unit can be refitted in the reverse manner.

REPLACING BULBS

Sidelamp and Front-direction Indicator Bulbs. The side lights and front-direction indicators are similar units using a single-filament bulb. These bulbs can be removed after unscrewing the two screws securing the appropriate lens in position, and turning the bulb slightly anti-clockwise. Offset pins are fitted to these bulbs to prevent incorrect installation, and if difficulty is experienced in installing these bulbs, they

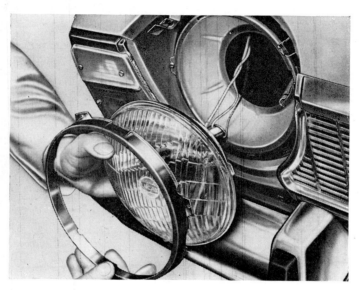

61. RENEWING SEALED-BEAM HEADLAMP UNIT

Illustration shows lamp unit and inner bezel.

Access to lamp unit is gained after removing outer bezel (retained by two bolts at bottom and two crosshead screws at top) and inner bezel (retained by three crosshead screws). Do not touch the two slotted screws as these control the headlamp alignment.

Lift out the unit and disconnect the plug.

envelope of the bulb and only the complete unit can be replaced.

To remove a headlamp unit, unscrew the two bolts at the bottom of the outer bezel and the two crosshead screws located towards the top of the bezel. Lift off the bezel and seal. Once the outer bezel has been removed, the inner bezel which retains the light unit in position can be seen; this inner bezel is retained by three cross-head screws. Two slotted screws can also be seen, these control the headlamp alignment and should not be touched. Remove the three cross-head screws and the inner bezel, when the unit can be removed and the wiring disconnected by pulling the plug off the back of the reflector.

After connecting the plug to the three pins

should be withdrawn from the holder, turned through half a turn and refitted. Before fitting the lens, ensure that the gasket is correctly located on its rear face to make a watertight joint, install the lens and retain it with the two screws.

Rear-direction Indicator and Rear/Stop-lamp Bulbs. The rear/stop lamp and rear direction-indicator lamp-bulb holders are retained in the lamp bodies by spring clips. To change a bulb from inside the luggage compartment, ease the bulb holder out of the back of the lamp. The bulbs are normal bayonet fitting (as side-lamp bulbs). To ensure correct alignment of the bulbs, the bulb holders are located in the lamp body by a tongue which aligns with a slot on the

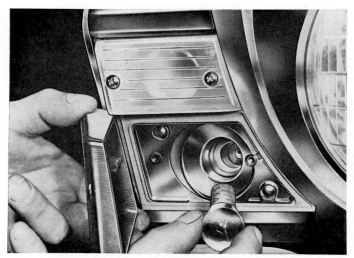

62. RENEWING FRONT-DIRECTION INDICATOR BULB

To replace a front-direction indicator bulb, take off the lens secured by two screws. Then turn bulb slightly anticlockwise and remove.

To prevent incorrect replacement of the new bulb, offset pins are used. When refitting the lens, ensure the gasket is correctly located to provide a watertight joint.

The sidelamp bulb is replaced in a similar manner.

bulb holder. Take care to align the bulb holder correctly when replacing it.

The lenses for these lamps can be removed as follows. Unscrew the crosshead screw from the bottom of the rear-lamp bezel and lift off the bezel. Remove the two screws which secure the upper retaining bar. Then remove the three screws securing the lenses to the body.

The rear-lamp diffuser, which illuminates the luggage boot, is exposed when the rear lenses have been removed. This is retained by four screws and, if it is being replaced, it should be fitted with the prisms facing into the luggage boot and towards the outside of the car.

When refitting the rear-lamp lenses, make sure the large gasket is correctly located behind them and the cork gasket fitted between the upper and lower lenses.

Mechanical Stop-lamp Switch. A mechanical stop-lamp switch is secured to the brake-pedal bracket, the operating plunger resting on the pedal shank. If this is replaced at any time, the position of the switch should be adjusted by means of the two retaining nuts so that the stop lamps are 'On' when the brake pedal is moved through $\frac{3}{16}$ to $\frac{5}{8}$ in.

Rear Number-plate Bulb. The rear number-plate bulb can be removed after first unscrewing

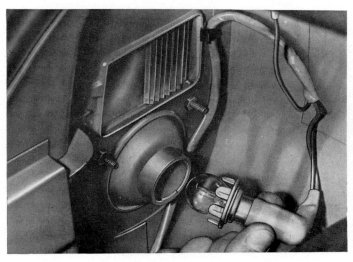

63. RENEWING COMBINED REAR AND STOP-LAMP BULBS

To replace the bulb from inside the luggage compartment, gently pull the bulb holder out of its reflector and then remove the bulb.

When refitting, note that the bulb holder is located in the lamp body by a tongue which registers with a space between the holder tabs.

The rear-direction indicator bulb is renewed in a similar manner.

the two crosshead screws securing the lens to the mounting bracket.

Interior Light. The interior light, where fitted, has a festoon-type bulb; this can be withdrawn from its retaining clips after removing the lamp lens, which is held in place by two screws passing into the lamp base.

Instrument Panel Bulbs. The warning and panel-lamp bulbs are bayonet type fitted in bulb holders located in the instrument panel. To renew these bulbs, it is necessary to remove the instrument panel. To do this, remove the three securing screws from the inner face of the panel shroud and lift off the shroud which is located by pegs at the front edge. Unscrew the speedometer-cable retaining nut and withdraw the cable. The panel is held in place by three screws passing through brackets at either end of the panel and on the back of the speedometer; remove these screws and lift the panel forwards and upwards – disconnect the multi-pin plug from the panel.

The panel and warning-lamp bulbs are fitted in plastic holders located in the back of the panel. Turn the bulb holder a quarter turn anticlockwise, lift out the bulb holder and remove the bulb. A printed circuit is used for the electrical circuit on the instrument panel and metal inserts in the bulb holders make the necessary contacts when these are refitted. When replacing the instrument panel, the multi-pin plug is located by a key and cannot be refitted incorrectly.

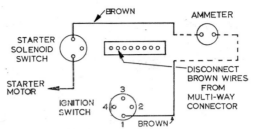

64. CONNECTIONS FOR FITTING AMMETER

It is advisable to carry always one spare bulb of each type so that, if failure occurs on the road, this can be replaced immediately.

It is now an offence to operate a vehicle on the road at any time of the day if the obligatory lights are inoperative and spare side, rear and number-plate bulbs should be carried.

FITTING AUXILIARY FOG OR DRIVING LAMP

If an auxiliary fog or driving lamp is fitted, their switches should be wired through the ignition-switch terminal No. 2 as shown by the dotted lines in the wiring diagram. If the lamp is to be used for normal driving, the centre of the lamp must be mounted 24 in. above the surface of the road. Provided the lamp is only used in fog or other conditions of bad visibility, it can be set at any height.

FITTING AMMETER

Should you wish to fit a separate ammeter,

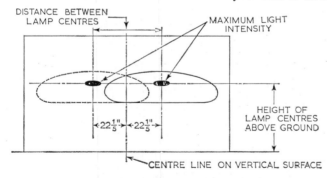

65. LIGHT PATTERN TO BE OBTAINED WHEN SETTING HEADLAMP BEAMS

The car should be positioned, unladen, on a level surface with its centre line on the centre line of the vertical surface and ten feet away from it.

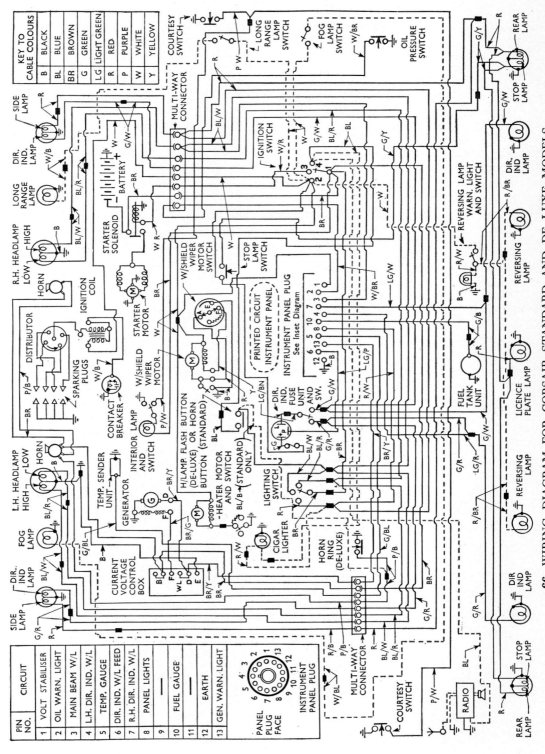

KEY TO CABLE COLOURS

B	BLACK
BL	BLUE
BR	BROWN
G	GREEN
LG	LIGHT GREEN
R	RED
P	PURPLE
W	WHITE
Y	YELLOW

PIN NO.	CIRCUIT
1	VOLT STABILISER
2	OIL WARN. LIGHT
3	MAIN BEAM W/L
4	L.H. DIR. IND. W/L
5	TEMP. GAUGE
6	DIR. IND. W/L FEED
7	R.H. DIR. IND. W/L
8	PANEL LIGHTS
9	—
10	FUEL GAUGE
11	EARTH
12	—
13	GEN. WARN. LIGHT

66. WIRING DIAGRAM FOR CORSAIR STANDARD AND DE LUXE MODELS

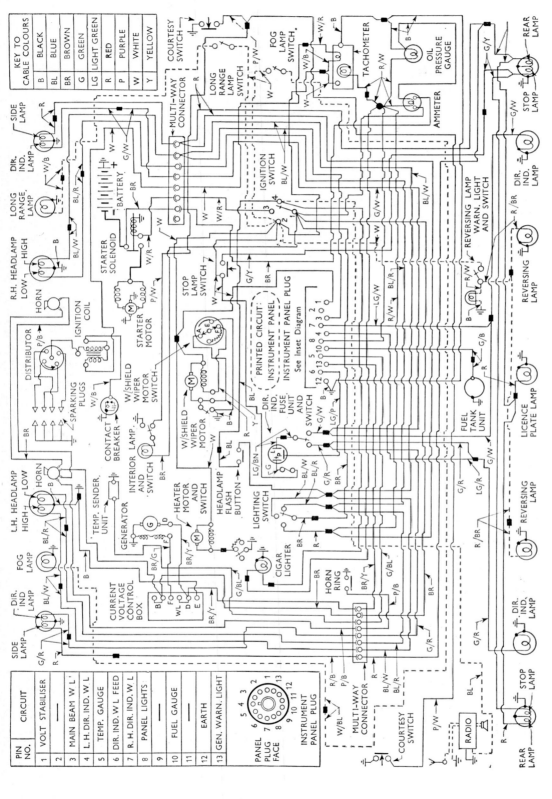

67. WIRING DIAGRAM FOR CORSAIR G.T.

KEY TO CABLE COLOURS	
B	BLACK
BL	BLUE
BR	BROWN
G	GREEN
LG	LIGHT GREEN
R	RED
P	PURPLE
W	WHITE
Y	YELLOW

PIN NO.	CIRCUIT
1	VOLT STABILISER
2	
3	MAIN BEAM W L'
4	L.H. DIR. IND. W L
5	TEMP. GAUGE
6	DIR. IND. W L FEED
7	R.H. DIR. IND. W L
8	PANEL LIGHTS
9	
10	FUEL GAUGE
11	EARTH
12	
13	GEN. WARN. LIGHT

this must be wired in series with the black-red wire from the starter-solenoid switch which goes to the ignition-switch terminal No. 1. This can be done by disconnecting the two black-red wires at the multi-way connector and inserting the ammeter leads between them as shown in Fig. 64.

If the ammeter shows a discharge when the engine is running, simply reverse the connections on the back of the ammeter.

ADJUSTING HEADLAMP ALIGNMENT

The headlamp alignment is best checked on the special equipment available for this purpose, but if necessary, it can be checked in the following manner.

On a suitable vertical surface mark a line at the same height from the ground as the centre of the headlamps. Through this horizontal line mark a vertical centre line and two other vertical lines 22·2 in. on either side of the centre line. The car should be positioned, unladen, on a level surface with its centre line on the centre line of the vertical surface and ten feet away from it. Remove the headlamp bezel and the headlamp alignment can now be adjusted by means of the vertical and horizontal adjustment screws located at the top and side of the headlamp body.

The bright spot of each headlamp should fall on the intersection of the horizontal line and the two vertical lines. This adjustment may be made easier by coverting each headlamp in turn and adjusting the other one.

DIRECTION INDICATORS

The direction indicators are controlled by the switch on the right-hand side of the steering column and incorporate a 5-amp fuse in the circuit. If the direction indicators do not work at any time, the fuse should be checked, after removing it from its plastic bayonet-type holder. If the fuse is satisfactory and the direction indicators are still inoperative, the flasher unit itself may be faulty. This is a round metal cylinder, rather similar in appearance to a radio valve, and is secured to the instrument panel by one bolt passing through a bracket on one end, the wiring being connected to it by a plug which locates on the three pins in the flasher unit. A blown flasher bulb is indicated by the unit ticking faster than normal and if this is heard the bulbs should be checked.

WINDSCREEN WIPER MOTOR

The variable-speed electric wiper motor fitted normally requires no maintenance.

INDEX